THE ADVENTURES OF AN ECONOMIC MIGRANT

Anthony Wade

Ian Randle Publishers
Kingston • Miami

First published in Jamaica, 2007 by
Ian Randle Publishers
11 Cunningham Avenue
Box 686
Kingston 6
www.ianrandlepublishers.com

© 2007 Anthony Wade

ISBN 987-976-637-339-9 (hardback)

ISBN 978-976-637-338-2 (paperback)

A catalogue record for this book is available from the National Library
of Jamaica

Cover photo by Lorenzo Henry
Cover and book design by Ian Randle Publishers

Printed in Great Britain

A	B	C	D	E	F	G	H

I	J	K	L	M	N	P	Q

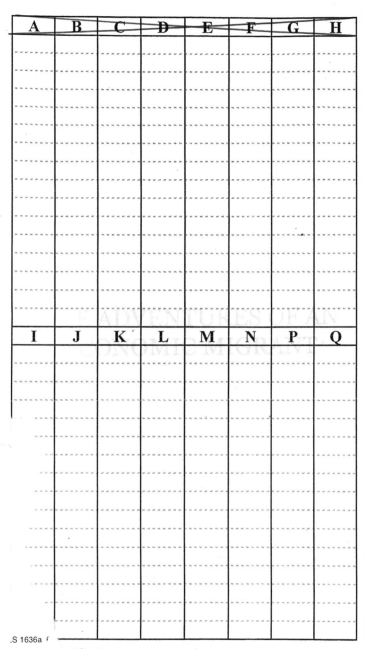

.S 1636a

Daphne the lady who changed the course of my life

Dedicated to the memory of my parents,
James Nicholas and Anne Wade

Contents

Acknowledgements... ix

Foreword... x

Introduction.. xiii

1. Reflections on Montserrat... 1

2. The Trek from Morning Hill.. 17

3. Encounters in a New Land.. 23

4. The Enterprise Mantle.. 36

5. Community Development.. 40

6. In Love for the First Time... 45

7. A Testing Time... 51

8. Messages from across the Sea... 53

9. Reunited... 56

10. Building an Industry... 67

11. The Corporate Animal.. 78

12. A Cricket Bat... 97

13. A Celebration.. 100

14. The Succession.. 103

15. The (UK) Caribbean Chamber of Commerce..............   105

16. The Private Sector.....................................   113

17. New Businesses and Community Development.........   118

18. A Second Chance With Love........................   128

19. An Invitation To Buckingham Palace   133

20. North London Training and Enterprise
     Council (TEC)...   137

21. A Merger that went Wrong...........................   144

22. Defeating The 'Young Turks'.......................   152

23. Love for a Third Time..............................   157

24. New River Health Authority.......................   168

25. The Redevelopment of Stonebridge.............   172

26. The Montserrat Volcano Trust Fund...........   187

27. Change in Ethnic Advancement.................   194

28. Winding Down   199

Appendix I.   Selection of Congratulations...................   207

Appendix II.   Music Sheets And Treasured Moments....   213

Acknowledgements

What next? This question from many people has been a powerful influence in prompting me to write this book. I therefore owe a huge debt of gratitude to all those people who have been my source of strength as I recaptured moments in my journey that stretched far and wide from the tiny island of Montserrat to many parts of the world.

Along the way, there have been moments of joy and sorrow, moments of success and failure, moments of challenge that called for courage, which helped to bring out the best in me. It is at moments like those that one may rejoice in the fact that one has the faith to confidently persevere and feel secure in pursuing one's goals. I owe such a debt to so many that it is quite impossible to name them all and I offer here a humble thank-you to all those who have given unstintingly of their time and their love to sustain me over the years from childhood to manhood.

In particular, I think of loved ones no longer with us, my parents and grandparents and other family members who nurtured and cared for me. The family bonding mechanism of caring shown by my uncles and aunts was manifestly an all–embracing safety net and sanctuary.

The priceless love, affection and support of my wives, my children, my brothers and sister have all, in their respective ways, been a huge umbrella of kindness. Blessings and love to you all.

Most important, this book would not have seen the light of day without the intelligent, critical appraisal of my dear wife Vasantha.

In conclusion, I want to say a big thank-you, first to my dear friends Cynthia Graham and Khalila Maragh for being my sounding board, and a big thank-you to my editor Dr Paulette Feraria for her patience in helping to make some sense of what I have had to say. Finally it has been difficult to disengage myself from some parts of my first book How They Made A Million to which I have been inextricably bound.

The journey continues and thus far it has been one full of fun, laughter and personal fulfillment, for which I give God thanks.

Hopefully, you too will find a laugh or two as you walk backwards with me.

Foreword
by Hon. Lascelles A. Chin O.J., C.D.

I got to know Tony Wade in the late eighties when we both became stakeholders in a triangular partnership in the Beauty Care Industry that stretched between Kingston, London and Chicago.

Tony's quiet, unassuming manner belies his accomplishments and leadership in the industry in the UK during the third quarter of the last century. His journey is remarkable as it unfolds. His influence on change in the industry is admirable and the opportunities he created for employment and advancement for the community are noteworthy. His leadership was felt, not only in his industry, but also at the grass roots, in community life and in public bodies.

In the foreword by Sir Bill Morris of Wade's earlier book *How They Made A Million: The Dyke & Dryden Story*, there is a paragraph that illustrates brilliantly the very essence of this remarkable story, which I quote below:

> 'If every journey of a thousand miles starts with one small step, then the achievements chronicled by Tony Wade in this book are as relevant as Neil Armstrong's journey to the moon.'

That quote reflects the formidable strength and character of the man in his lifelong crusade for the need to establish a black business enterprise presence in Britain, one in which his company has led the way.

Wade argues forcefully that much has been made of the glossy words of equal opportunity, a phrase adopted across the entire employment arena. It is a claim, he points out, that often overlooks the subtle distinction between equal opportunity and equal access. 'It is the lack of equal access,' he declares, 'that makes the going so tough on the black community.'

The Adventures of an Economic Migrant shows just how successful the author has been in inspiring others. His rise to the top of his business career to become a champion in his industry is a fascinating journey, filled with challenges and attainment driven by hard work and a solid commitment to service to others.

The book reveals, too, something of the inner man, of his Christian upbringing and the strength of his faith in adversity. It unfolds the multidimensional spirit of the adventurer, entrepreneur, campaigner and influencer that makes for such compelling reading.

-Lascelles Chin

and
by Rudi Page

Tony Wade has been for me an energizer. I have known him for 25 years, both as an employee and as a colleague. During that period our work embraced some of the many challenges that faced black communities as together we strived to influence change within our society.

In both the private and public sectors, his energy and fortitude have been of immense benefit to all communities to lead the development of an entire industry that today produces thousands of jobs is no mean achievement. His leadership role in his own generation and his own mentoring of the next have ensured that he command the respect of our whole community.

The Caribbean island of Montserrat, his birthplace, has also gained from his business skills, knowledge and networking, following the island's volcano disaster. He was instrumental in the formation of the Montserrat Volcano Fund and in re-establishing economic and cultural links with the Republic of Ireland.

As someone who knows him well, I recognise that his personal qualities of determination and discipline are the tenets by which he lives. He would always devise practical solutions, never giving up until objectives have been met. Some will agree that these are rare attributes in today's world. I would say without hesitation, that they are the hallmarks that set him apart from the rest.

Rudi Page
Statecraft Consulting Ltd
Cultural Knowledge Management

'Chemara'

Introduction

'Chemara', the retreat from which this book was written, lies deep in the garden parish of St Ann, fifteen minutes from one of Jamaica's most popular tourist attractions, the cascading Dunn's River Falls on the edge of the bustling town of Ocho Rios.

Gates facing east give access to a gradient that sweeps into a courtyard decked with Christmas palms and bougainvilleas on either side. Follow diamond-shaped stone paths left or right and you come upon a delightful bougainvillea hedge that overhangs a thirty-foot drop of concrete-reinforced stone wall rising from a gully below. During the rainy season the gully becomes a roaring watercourse that snakes along its well-worn path to the sea, while in dry times it remains a trail of adventure.

A rainforest-like cluster of trees, lush and stately, overlooks the western perimeter, home to a variety of butterflies and birds. Among the birds are snow-white cattle egrets with pink eyes and yellow bills, colourful hummingbirds, brown-crested doves, and tuneful-nightingales that fill the air with music.

'Chemara' nestles in the centre of an acre with a formal garden on the northern perimeter creatively crafted by my wife Vasantha. An African tulip takes pride of place in the centre of the lawn while graceful queen palms tower over pink, purple and sunset hibiscus. A variety of crotons add further to the rich mixture of colour, while traveller's palms and dwarf coconut trees form a picturesque backdrop to a gazebo and swimming pool.

An arrangement of heliconias and ginger lilies grouped along a steep pathway behind the kidney-shaped pool stands out in dazzling colour. Of special interest in this cluster of exotics, is the torch ginger's brilliant red.

On the southern side the garden is less formal, but equally interesting with its collection of handsomely patterned foliage of green and white cultivars together with cat's tails, mini-bamboo clusters, ferns and a hibiscus hedge which makes for a corner of quiet relaxation. There is a good collection of fruit trees among which the celebrated ackee, famous for its yolk-like vegetable delicacy, flourishes in abundance.

The ackee is unique. It is a fruit, yet is prepared and served as a vegetable. It takes pride of place served with codfish as the Jamaican national dish. The collection of fruits and vegetables in this part of the garden makes the quiet corner a most interesting place especially when fruits are in season.

It is particularly rewarding at harvest time to gather the fruits and vegetables one has planted—an exercise that makes one feel really close to nature. Getting the hands dirty provides a special kind of relaxation, contentment and peace of mind that can only be found in a garden. Gathering sugar apples (known as sweetsop in Jamaica), for example, recaptures for me boyhood days of adventure all the more so because I planted the seeds for the fruit I enjoy today.

Choice of the site can be credited to my wife. It was at one of my company's annual exhibitions that I bought into the idea offered by an exhibitor of acquiring land in Jamaica. I suggested that he contact Vasantha with his proposal for I knew she hated the cold and wanted to live in Jamaica where it is nice and warm all year round. Never have I seen her so excited! Before I knew it, she was on a plane to Jamaica to choose a site that I later visited. We were of the same mind. As usual, her choice could not be faulted.

No time was to be lost in getting our home project moving. In the same week arrangements were made with a construction company to produce plans to our specification. Contrary to warnings about dishonest contractors, our dealings with the company selected, L. Morris Construction Ltd, were entirely satisfactory.

Vasantha was a regular visitor to the project. She breathed down the builders' necks to ensure that their work was carried out in line with our plans and that her dream home was delivered as she had planned it. There were occasions when the builders were glad to see the back of her and would telephone me in London to complain.

The layout of the house was designed by Vasantha in a setting that allowed me to recapture some aspects of my journey across planet earth. 'Chemara', the name chosen for our home, has always been a subject of particular interest to our visitors.

Some guests have dubbed it the 'inside-outside place', the reason being that its layout with large, airy, light-filled windows, seems to draw you outside even while still inside, with views of the gardens from whatever angle you may choose.

In 1997, on a visit to Malaysia, we made what was for Vasantha a nostalgic trip to Chemara, a research station that was her childhood home. She was deeply moved. I suggested that our new home be named 'Chemara' to preserve the memory.

We have often been asked: Why Jamaica? The short answer is that the island is one of the most spectacularly beautiful places in the Caribbean. That aside, any of the other islands in the region could easily have become home to me, although Montserrat spiritually holds me in a fond embrace from which I can never escape and to which I return from time to time.

It was on June 21, 1954 that I boarded the SS *Ascania* and sailed for England. I have often referred to the journey as an 'adventure' that ended up in London. It has however turned out to be so much more: a fantastic experience in life's lessons that I could never have dreamed of.

It is virtually impossible to recapture all the lessons learned--nor will I try--but I hope *The Adventures of an Economic Migrant* will provide readers with snapshots of my past, in much the same way as it holds up a mirror to me as I write.

Reflections on
Montserrat

Montserrat—'The Other Emerald Isle'—can easily be described as an oasis of peace and tranquillity, set apart in a turbulent world. An extract from Exclusive Properties on Montserrat describes the island thus:

> 'A lush island so green it looks like a beautiful emerald lying in the crystal blue of the Caribbean Sea. High mountains rise from the centre of the island and taupe sand beaches fringe the leeward shores. The foothills are dotted with luxurious villas, surrounded by exotic tropical gardens, where fragrant blooms and fruit-laden trees overload your senses.'

While that statement is all very true, it is however worlds apart from the places that I roamed as a boy to which I am about to take you on a stroll with me down memory lane.

Davy Hill and Morning Hill, in northern Montserrat, the place where I was born and grew up as a boy, shaped my character and remains for me a sanctuary of precious memories. It is the one place on earth that wraps me in a fond embrace, even when I am thousands of miles away from the 39½ square mile dot of an island planted by Nature in the Caribbean Sea. It retains, for me, a magnetic spiritual pull.

Sealed deep in the vault of a graphic boyhood memory are fond recollections of the past. Vivid scenes remain of the island masqueraders that delighted the senses as they wound their way dancing along crowded streets of the north, ending up in the village of St. John's on Boxing Day. Occasionally, as they danced along the streets, boys and girls were sometimes held hostage by 'horned devils', until their parents placed a payment in the masqueraders' 'pot' for their release.

Their costumes were fascinating. Bright, flowing robes decorated with multicoloured ribbons; small mirrors of various shapes and sizes shimmered and dazzled in the bright sunshine as the troupe danced to the rhythm of the boom-drum, fife and shac-shac (maracas).

New Year's Day saw the climax of the celebrations, as crowds made their way into Plymouth for the bumper party. Parades of masqueraders, among them guppies adorned in flowery apparel moved along the narrow, winding streets of the town with cheering crowds in tow conjuring up a picture of the Pied Piper of Hamelin. No one had a care in the world; these were moments of fun to savour.

Never far away along memory lane, was the foul sulphur smell drifting over the town from the island's volcano. The Soufriere Hills' glowing mountain furnace of 1997 and its subsequent actions have caught the attention of the world, bringing to the island the world's best seismic minds to unravel its erratic behaviour.

The awesome destructive power of this sleeping earth-encrusted, once dormant 'demon', has also inspired an abundance of literary and artistic talent to capture its roaring fury in verse and song. 'Seismic Glow', a CD by 'Zunky N' Dem', relates in graphic detail the horrors of its mighty explosion that claimed the lives of many and left once vibrant communities desolate.

Kathy Buffonge's book in three volumes, *A Chronicle of Montserrat's Volcanic Experience*, covers the eventful years of 1995, 1996 and 1997 with Sir Howard Fergus' *'Fiftieth Anniversary Anthology of Poems'*, celebrating the University of the West Indies, and Montserratian Hope during a Volcanic Crisis together convey the national mood over the devastation and make for sober reading.

Ten years later, the July 2005 Soufriere Hills International Scientific Conference on the island, attended by the world's elite seismologists, would still be in 'conjecture mode' as to the behavioural patterns of the 'demon'.

These comments by Professor Sparks of Bristol University are mind-boggling to say the least: 'What we found was that Montserrat had a very small number of eruptions over the last hundred thousand years, perhaps six or seven big eruptions, and this was one of them.'

Sparks went on to conclude that six or seven major eruptions in one hundred thousand years 'means there had to be an average of twenty thousand years of absolutely nothing happening.' This picture

2

of Montserratians literally living and walking with the 'demon' all through the generations simply blows the mind!

Steeped in Irish tradition, I had never quite understood what brought about my hybrid inheritance of two shared cultures. Part Irish and part African/Montserratian, it was always a puzzle that my surname Wade bears no resemblance to my African heritage. I was later to discover the surname was an imposition on my forefathers during slavery, among the ugliest and most degrading of crimes inflicted on members of the human race.

The enforced Irish connection and origin of the name Wade can be traced to the Oriel counties in Ireland, dating back to 1066 where it was first registered in the Domesday Book.

Records show in the Oriel counties, that MacWade is a corruption of MacQuaid. Elsewhere, Wade is of dual derivation, old English waddan, to go, and Norman-French Wade, ford—and has appeared in all provinces since the thirteenth century. Quite a discovery for a local lad!

It is reported that thirty per cent of all original European surnames sported a coat of arms. In the Wade case, it was represented by an Asure, a saltire between four *escalopes d'or*. The crest: Rhinoceros Argent. Its Motto: *in spe resto*-Stand firm in hope. It was a thought not far removed from my father's dictum: 'always think positively.' Was there a connection, I wondered?

This discovery came quite by accident, and was spotted by my children while we were holidaying in Gibraltar. It brought about a chance purchase after some gentle persuasion to part with £35.00, which at the time I could ill-afford. It gave me, however, a glimpse into the history of a name that is of purely academic interest.

It was the Irish settlers coming in 1632 whose influence, after mixing with their slaves prevailed. They left their mark on the island in a multitude of ways that determined the duality of my heritage.

My father, as his skin colour indicated, was positively of mixed Irish blood, the result of some liaison between Irish masters and their African female slaves. But there could be no mistaking my mother's heritage. She was indisputably a darling 'black sugar' of pure African stock.

After years of fighting with the French, the British finally claimed Montserrat in 1783. Settlers were mostly displaced Irish, thrown out of Ireland by Oliver Cromwell. The island is known as 'The Other Emerald Isle' perhaps because of its topography that reminded the settlers of the places they had left behind. It is no accident, therefore, that almost all place names and surnames on the island are of Irish origin.

The Shamrock embellishes your Montserrat passport as you stride through immigration. Such very distinctive Irish emblems, as 'the lady of the harp' are symbols that feature prominently in the national life of the island. Government House had the distinction of being the only place where the Union Jack and the Irish Tricolour flew side by side, another manifestation of the island's Irishness.

The annual St. Patrick's Day holiday, March 17, very much a part of the Irish tradition in celebration of its patron saint, is embraced and shared by islanders to a large degree. But then there is the failed slave revolt on that very date in 1768 by the island's black 'freedom fighters'. The coincidence of a dual celebration with widely different interpretations is not difficult to understand!

These historical links with Ireland are important for both countries, especially in finding expression for cultural exchanges, since a huge amount of Montserrat's history is to be found in Irish archives. Centuries-old sugar mills around the island are poignant reminders of the slave labour of past generations.

From everything that has been said, the connected heritage is not in doubt. Howard Fergus in his *Montserrat: Emerald Isle of the Caribbean* tells us:

> 'Montserrat had Irish colonists for its early settlers and Montserratians to this day have the Connaught brogue curiously engrafted on the African jargon. It is said that a Connaught man, on arriving at Montserrat, was, to his astonishment, hailed in vernacular Irish by a black man from one of the first boats that came alongside. "Thunder and turf", exclaimed Pat, "how long have you been here? Three months! And so black already!" "Hanum a diaul," says Pat, thinking Quashie a countryman, "I'll not stay among ye." And in a few hours the Connaught man was on his return, with his white skin, to the Emerald Isle.'

There is a body of opinion which insists that it is not too late in the day to ask for reparations from a prosperous Ireland. It is argued that this will go a long way towards healing some of the terrible wounds inflicted on the people of Montserrat. This body of opinion is also aware of a grim irony. The Irish settlers were themselves refugees fleeing from English persecution but, shamefully, they too perpetrated slave crimes. While reparations will not cure the racially inflicted wounds of slavery, acknowledgement of the crimes of past Irish settlers will help the process of healing and forgiveness for the deep-seated hurt of our ancestors.

While some Montserratians see their immediate claim to be on Ireland, black peoples across the diaspora have been victims of the slave trade. The countries of Europe who engaged in, and benefited from the trade, should feel obliged in the name of conscience for the wrongs committed by their predecessors, and should subscribe to a 'reparation' fund – perhaps not in cash but in kind.

Two hundred years on, the perpetuation of the effectual damage from the savagery of slavery on our forbears still lingers, manifesting itself in numerous ways. Low self-esteem still prevails and the inability of millions of our people to shake off the deep-seated hurt of the crime that robs a proud people of its dignity. It is fashionable for young adults of our current generation to change their surnames to disassociate themselves from the nagging reminder of a disgraced, inherited human legacy. My own children have changed their names for that reason.

In a bold and statesmanlike manner, Prime Minister Blair in October 2001 correctly and courageously raised the plight of Africa when he asserted that '...the state of Africa is a scar on the conscience of the world' and subsequently acted on his statement which has been applauded by all the nations concerned.

In 2006, with the approach of the bicentennial anniversary of slavery in 2007, the matter was raised in the House of Commons by Mr Blair but he however stopped short of discussing a formula to make amends. Were he to take on board the moral leadership of putting to rest the vexed question of reparation, this could very well add significantly to his laurels and stature as a true humanitarian leader in the contemporary world affairs of the twenty-first century.

I cannot help feeling that Caribbean leadership has been painfully slow, and less than resolute, in putting on the table the issue of reparation—especially as there are precedents to follow. Israel is, perhaps, the classic case of deserved reparation from the evil of Nazism and slavery, one of the most heinous of crimes perpetrated by one group of humans against another, should be dealt with no differently.

In 2007, it is my fervent hope that Caribbean nations will celebrate and mark this bicentenary of freedom from slavery appropriately, in ways that will remain pillars of strength, and signal hope that future generations will never again have to endure enslavement.

Many extraordinary stories exist about the Irish settlers on Montserrat; listening to some of them has been an astonishing experience. Tales of jumbie dancers in the moonlight on Morning Hill or the sighting of Irish ghosts quarrelling and eventually duelling over the theft of slaves and sugar plantations of long ago never cease to fascinate. There are too, folk tales of gold bullion buried deep in the hillsides of Morning Hill and guarded by a patrol of Irish ghosts.

It was reported that the Irish were partial to rum and imbibed huge quantities of the stuff. One of the places where the ghosts hung out was said to be on Bay River Bridge, a short distance away from the hillside where the gold bullion was supposed to have been buried. After getting drunk, a favourite ghost's pastime, it was claimed, was to sing and dance on the bridge in the moonlight. These scary stories were enough to prevent any of us children from ever crossing that bridge once it got dark.

Stories abound of regular sightings by village people, of huge balls of fire darting 'with lightning speed' from one hilltop to another, reappearing in seconds and repeating this at intervals during the night. These unexplained occurrences were referred to as 'jack-o-lanterns' and left one shaking with fear for days after a sighting.

A lone traveller tells of what happened late one night on his way home. He was mysteriously swooped upon by a huge 'jack-o-lantern' that forced him to run for shelter to the nearest house at 'Sweeneys', where he found refuge from an awesome ball of fire. The 'demonic evil spirit', it was said, continued to surround the house till morning before it disappeared.

Of the many ghost stories that existed, none was perhaps more intriguing than the custom of the 'jumbie table' that takes place on December 24. A white linen tablecloth, it was said, covered a table set with an assortment of special treats enjoyed by past loved ones during their lifetime. Folk tale has it that, once the table was set, there could be no interference with the feast until next morning after the table was cleared. Anyone who attempted to interfere did so at his or her peril!

A cultural tradition of 'jumbie dances' prevailed, which led dancers to get into a trance and communicate with spirits from the

6

past who, it is said, had all kinds of magical powers including the ability to heal the sick.

Talking drums, fifes, fiddles and shac-shacs were the musical instruments that blasted melodies to set dancers moving first in slow motion and then, as the event progressed, sending them leaping and diving into a spinning and twirling frenzy when, it is said, the trance took place and exchanges with the ghosts began.

Dances usually carried on from sunset right through the night till morning, but might also last for days once the spirits were let loose and appetites were lubricated with gallons of rum.

One of these dances, it is claimed, was called for when a 16-year-old girl, on her way home with a pig, complained of a severe headache. On reaching the church gate at St John's, her pig mysteriously dropped dead! She was said to have 'heard voices talking to her'. Medical attention was sought, but her condition worsened. A 'jumbie dance' was organised for her during which time she was healed.

In an interview on Sunday May 21, 2005 in London with an 89-year-old lady about ghost stories on the island, I questioned her about the story of the 'girl and pig' referred to above. To my amazement, she revealed to me, 65 years later, that she was that 16-year-old girl in the story. I found it difficult to believe that what I was hearing was true!

On Morning Hill, the sun in all its majesty always lighted up a glorious new day. From the hilltop, the sea seemed to kiss the horizon beyond while, dotted in the distance like pyramids, sat the neighbouring islands of Antigua, St Kitts, Nevis and the uninhabited bird sanctuary of Redondo.

Morning Hill at dawn was for me the greatest place to be. The music of birdsong, crowing cocks, chirping chickens, grunting pigs, donkeys braying, cows mooing and 'mountain chickens' (frogs) barking in the surrounding hills filled the air with an indescribable symphony.

As morning lengthened, a colony of bees could be seen busily searching for pollen, while a thousand shades of butterflies regally danced in the sunlight, making the place a paradise. As evening closed in, one could capture the beauty of a golden sunset fading over a low horizon, to signal the end of another perfect day on the hill.

Down the steep slopes of the hill, permanently placed gigantic volcanic rock formations, fashioned in the most amazing shapes were sights which only poets would dare to describe.

Quite often, as my brother and I negotiated the rocks down to the river on fruit-gathering expeditions, we could see snakes' heads popping out from under the rocks, only to slither in our direction along tracks in the hillside. Although I knew they were harmless, I would literally freeze, terrified at the sight of these twisting creatures.

The terrain lent itself in abundance to two kinds of fruit, sugar apples and soursops. In season, they provided a most welcome supplement to our daily vitamin intake.

At the bottom of the hill stood a huge hairy mango tree, whose every branch was crowded with the most delicious fruit and whose flavour you could inhale from some distance away. 'Speckled feasts' made for a great mango party. Nearly ripe mangoes were hand-picked to avoid bruising and placed in a bed of straw where they were left to mature until tiny speckles appeared on their skin, indicating that the mellowing process was complete and feasting could begin. These were wonderful mouth-watering occasions—a celebration of Nature's bounty.

Morning Hill was special. Distinctly cut off from the rest of the village, it was as it were, the village Great House. Its perimeter was decked with a variety of crotons, oleanders and lilies. What a pretty sight! On the outer edge of the perimeter was a splendid collection of cacti, assembled like menacing warders to issue a stern warning to keep away or suffer the pain that their millions of needles could inflict on contact.

The cactus family included the dreaded gall-like aloe plant, which was used medicinally for deworming children. It was revoltingly bitter and when its slimy green liquid was extracted, a pinch of salt would be added and the potion administered. In my time, I have had my fair share of the potion that seems to have done wonders in keeping me worm-free.

The thick green pulp of the aloe was also crushed and used as a shampoo and conditioner. This was a truly magnificent natural product that could always be relied upon for superb results in making the hair soft and pliable. The plant is, today, part of the 'back to Eden' philosophy, and is an ingredient of a multitude of skin-care preparations.

The matriarch of Morning Hill Great House, Kiziah Greenaway, was my grandmother. She always wore a welcoming smile and had the knack of putting one at ease with effortless charm. She was the greatest Granny ever, always gentle and kind, yet a firm disciplinarian.

This strength of character held her nine offsprings together, three boys and six girls. After the passing of my grandfather in 1925, she took charge, inspiring and guiding her children with the strong principles of her religious teachings.

While all her children have been a credit to her, two of her sons, my uncles Charles and Dick, made her particularly proud, attaining the highest levels of achievement in the teaching profession. Charles, as Headmaster of Cavalla Hill School was credited with an MBE for turning out the first crop of home-grown island administrators, while Dick made his mark as an inspector of schools. These gifted men were also Methodist local preachers and were respected for their influence in strengthening the family tradition of worshipping Methodists.

The annual Christmas pilgrimage to Morning Hill was, for my many cousins and members of the Greenaway clan, one of the great occasions we looked forward to as we grew up. It was a time we always remembered as we continued to keep the tradition alive in our respective families.

Generous servings of roast suckling pig with cassava bread stuffing and chitterlings followed by fancy cakes, were washed down with plentiful helpings of home-made brews of ginger beer or sorrel. The grown-ups' tipple, on the other hand, was wines of choice, while the privilege of youth was to sniff the corks!

Granny earned the undivided love and respect of her clan and indeed of the whole village, many of whom visited regularly to seek her wise counsel on matters they were unable to resolve themselves.

The custom of calling someone a name that differs from what appears on the birth certificate is quite peculiar and found to be the case island wide. It led me to my own version of that Shakespearian question: What is a name? and to my answer, a badge, a label used as an identity attached to a person or thing.

As it happens I have had the fortune--or misfortune--to carry a number of labels or badges. Registered at birth as Anthony Edward Samuel Wade, I came to abandon that name. I was registered at school as Harold Wade and known by all and sundry as such, (apart from my nickname of Parson). It was not until arrangements to travel were made that this peculiarity was rectified.

Confusion brought about by this name change was never far away. 'Hi Harold' was the way my friends would greet me, to which I would respond: 'I am not Harold anymore but Anthony'. Then the questions would follow. It did not end there; Anthony soon became Tony, the name that has stuck, except for official documentation purposes. Amused persons have often wondered which name is my alibi.

Responding about this peculiarity, my father explained that the names were a result of dreams. Some long gone relative with that name had appeared in a dream producing the new name, which it was assumed, was some kind of 'wish list' that parents felt they were obliged to pass on to their children.

My father became a lone parent after the passing of our mother at a relatively young age. He was not only the greatest dad, but was also our best friend. To his credit, he instinctively understood the golden rules of fatherhood, adequately providing his children with all that was necessary for our healthy development—a good home, proper clothing, plenty of fresh food and lots of love.

We had great fun with him. We each had our chores and were happy to carry them out without having to be reminded or cajoled into doing them. I have never once seen my father angry. On his shopping trips to Plymouth, he would diligently put aside the best of the goodies from his shopping expedition for us. Coconut tarts and sweet bread from Walkers of Salem, which he knew we loved, were always included in our packs.

On his fishing trips, the prized trunkfish from every catch was always reserved for us. The fun began on discovering that some were in the basket, as starters before our main meal. They were gutted, washed and seasoned then roasted on charcoal, after which we would all nibble away at our pre-prandial delicacy.

He was as generous as he could be with our pocket money, and always somehow exercised caution in handing it out by striking a fine balance between giving too much thus risking turning us into spendthrifts and too little, ensuring that we would think twice before blowing it. Before handing out the dollars, he would always say: 'First of all let me consult my little Barclays.' This was a savings box named after the bank he used for his financial transactions.

He was a man of independent means and instilled in his children the merits of thrift and the importance of positive thinking.

'Be smart', was his motto, a kind of inculcation in counselling his children. These words have remained ever present in my thoughts throughout my journeying. His implied meaning was that one should think and act positively at all times. This dictum has been my guiding principle, as will become evident throughout the pages in this book.

His skills were many, among them carpentry. He built his own house and crafted all his furniture of which he was justly proud. He was also a specialist boat builder and the owner of two boats. One he managed himself as a fisherman, the other he hired out and shared in the profits it generated.

As a farmer, he owned some fertile lands, several acres of which were devoted to growing sea-island cotton, while other areas were allocated to the cultivation of vegetables. These also brought in good returns, which made for a secure and dignified existence for himself and his children.

Cultivating cotton was his major investment activity. Montserrat sea-island cotton was the region's finest quality lint, branded 'MSI'. It was one of the island's premier exports. Garments that carried the MSI label were only to be found in stores noted for quality in the UK, North America and other parts of the world.

At crop time, our home was littered from floor to ceiling with pearly white lint. A good crop usually used up every square inch of the space allocated to cotton cleaning and preparation for bagging, before being sold for export. Unfortunately, this prized product has long been out of production and remains a great loss to the island's economy.

'Papa Nick' or 'Captain Nick' short for Nicholas, were the names by which my father was affectionately greeted. He shared a remarkable relationship with people of all walks of life and always got the very best out of his employees. His communication and entrepreneurial skills have without doubt left their mark on our village, for many villagers emulated the way he managed his labour relations and were well pleased with the way he dealt with people.

My sister-in-law, Gwendolyn Wade, tells a story of my father that is very revealing of his affection for my mother. On her first visit to Montserrat with my brother John to meet her father-in-law, she found what she thought was a weird and unwelcoming attitude in my father. 'He looked me over from head to toe without saying a word,' she declared.

The next day, he greeted me with the following explanation. 'My dear, I guess you must have questioned my strange behaviour.' 'I wondered,' Gwendolyn replied. 'Well', he continued, 'I thought I saw a ghost, my son's mother.' He turned to his son and ordered him to take good care of me.

I have fond childhood memories of my dearest mother. I recall her always singing. She was recognised as a fine singer throughout the village and beyond. The love and warmth of her hugs and the sound of her voice as she sang one of her favourite hymns lingers on and remains to this day ever fresh in my memory.

In heavenly love abiding,
No change my heart shall fear;
And safe is such confiding,
For nothing changes here:
The storm may roar without me,
My heart may low be laid;
But God is round about me,
And can I be dismayed?"

The hymn must somehow have been sublimely implanted into my subconscious, for it is one of the things that have stayed with me during those tender years, has had a profound effect on me in nurturing my own faith and has remained a source of great strength throughout my journey.

My grandparents on both sides of the family tree were a loving and close-knit family of wonderful people, always there for their grand children. 'Dardy', as we lovingly called my paternal grandfather, was always fun to be with. He taught me how to ride Roger, his handsome brown specimen of a horse whose coat glowed reflecting the care and attention Dardy gave him. Roger's mane and bushy tail were brushed daily and his hoofs shoed regularly to protect their soft underside. I was allowed to take him to the beach from time to time for bathing and especially enjoyed galloping him home through the village.

My grandfather taught me many things among them how to operate his cassava mill to do the milling; how to use the press that drained the milk from the cassava used for making starch and then collect the flour which was put through a drying process in the sun. After all these many processes, the flour then became my grandmother's property, from which she baked sheets of cassava bread on a flat cast-iron plate over a coal fire. At times she would add desiccated coconut to the mixture to make the bread a rare treat.

Apart from her baking, Grandma was a superb cook. The aroma from her kitchen, when wafted by the wind, was often inhaled for miles around the village, especially when she was cooking corned pork stew and black-eye peas.

Corned pork was usually prepared by salting and smoking the

pork over a coal fire with cinnamon leaves to enhance the flavour. This preparation made the stew even more tantalising to the taste buds and more so when she added dumplings made from a mixture of cassava flour and plain white flour. It was finger-licking good!

Our village was usually a tranquil place, but its peace was interrupted during the day by heavy trucks and cars negotiating the climb up the steep hill. Sometimes at nights, a lively burst of choruses from the local Pentecostal Church in the village livened up the place. These choruses were infectious and seemed to have an addictive effect on some worshippers, for on the following day, or even days later as you walked along the street or track, you would still hear some of the choruses that have been sung on previous nights.

Wandering down memory lane and recapturing a glimpse of boyhood pursuits refreshes the soul and provides great moments of the laughter and fun we shared. Imitating the island's defence force and pretending to be soldiers, singing war songs and parading with sticks and makeshift rifles in readiness to defend the mother country during World War II was real enough for us boys in the village.

As a seven-year-old then, nothing could have been further from my thoughts than that fourteen years later I would find myself part of the UK work force in the rebuilding of its economy. More about this later, but in the meantime our pranks and carefree lives moved on apace.

Collecting wild honey offered a boyhood experience for me and my friends Peter and Mark to laugh about. After slipping on our protective clothing, we bravely headed for a nearby hillside where there was a well-known beehive. We soon came face to face with the tempting honeycombs in the hive that made our mouths water, but were suddenly attacked by bees that somehow got under our masks.

We flew out of the cave screaming with the bees attacking us as we tried to discard our clothing. We were stung everywhere but our faces in particular were a sorry mess. It was the kind of ordeal you would not wish on your worst enemy.

The village meeting place for its teenagers was strategically positioned on and around 'Bigstone', a huge half-moon-shaped rock at the top of the village. Moonlit nights with twinkling stars above always brought out new creative talents in the group.

Items at these teenage gatherings were always improvised, consisting of story telling and calypso serenades. Singing in rounds was a great favourite. Examples included the catchy tunes of 'Row,

row, row your boat gently down the stream', 'Three blind mice' and 'Kookaburra sits in the old gum tree'. Negro spirituals were sung with gusto, as many a young crooner tried to outdo the other. Any opportunity for name-tagging was also a popular pastime. Say something odd and you were sure to be tagged.

An elderly man explaining how he saw a pig fly during a hurricane was promptly tagged 'Flying pig'—a name he hated. He would vent his fury on anyone who dared to hail him as such. Knowledge of this served only to add a chorus of 'Flying pig' by teenage boys wherever he was seen.

I must admit that I too could not resist the temptation of teasing him, but always made sure I was out of sight when I did! My father would not be amused, for he always taught us to respect our elders.

Nights on 'Bigstone' were also memorable for a variety of jokes, clean ones and rude ones. Some were distinctly original. The story of a Mr 'Bimbo Long Legs' told of someone of substantial means who returned to the island from the Panama Canal, his mouth decorated with gold and, it was said, was always flashing golden smiles. He soon became the toast of the ladies and was dubbed the local stud. His fortune, it was claimed, soon vanished when he invested in 'hairy banks' after which he was flat broke. In a desperate attempt to maintain his lifestyle he came up with an 'all-purpose' medicinal tablet formula, which made miracle claims as a cure for various ailments instantly. His advertised claims were: 'it cleans the bowels', 'makes you tell the truth' and 'improves the memory'.

A little old lady hearing his claims, ordered a double supply before stocks ran out. Delighted to put her hands on this wonder, she swallowed one tablet instantly and in a matter of minutes she started to vomit.

The man who was standing by beamed broadly. 'You see, just as I said, it cleans the bowels'. Recovering from her violent bout of vomiting, the old lady remarked, 'But it tastes like shit". The old man beamed even broader and yelled: 'You see, it makes you tell the truth'.

'Good God', screamed the old lady, looking the old man in the face. 'I will never forget you till the day I die.' Great! 'Now you'll have a super memory', chuckled the old man, 'just as I promised you would!'

Teenage fantasizing about our future was a regular feature at the gathering. These included serious matters such as a possible profession or the kind of vocation we might pursue. Finding ideal marriage partners was a subject not missed in our youthful conversing.

These were matters that were perhaps somewhat advanced considering our ages but, looking back, one thing was clear: reverence for the institution of marriage reflected standards set by our parents and by the influence of our society generally.

I recall my own thoughts on the subject. My ideal partner, I fancied, would be a nurse, for I was captivated by the kindly characteristics of nurses and their stylish uniforms. Another condition of this boyhood fantasy was that she should also be good at playing the piano. Nor would I ever consider marrying someone's daughter unless I had a home of my own to take her into. These were big ideas at that age—it was going to be interesting to see how this boyhood daydreaming materialized!

Our sporting ambitions were regularly aired and as you have guessed, every boy wanted to be a cricketer. Cricketing heroes like Sir Learie Constantine or George Headley were idols we revered. We contrived primitive bats from coconut branches, made do with oranges, grapefruit and indeed any fruit that might be used as balls. Play would take place anywhere a makeshift pitch could be put together, on the beach, in the street or on any suitable wasteland that could be found. The thing was to be able to time the ball and whack it as hard as you could, quite unorthodox perhaps, but great fun in those formative years.

Generally, a variety of team games were encouraged at school, aimed at building a competitive spirit. Among the games played were both long and high jumps, relays, tug-of-war, three-legged and flat races, all of which I excelled at, and was reputed 'to move like a gazelle'.

Sunday worship was the norm. Traditionally the church and the community were in many respects one big family. It was a vibrant and joyous interaction of caring and sharing. The church seasons, Christmas, Easter and Harvest were times of great rejoicing, not only for wearing your Sunday best, but also for giving God the best.

Our churches, I recall, did magnificent work and met many of the social needs within the community. Their work in the area of education stands out, and I am personally thankful for the early education I had from my local Methodist Church school.

My father was a good Christian and, as already noted, a multi-talented craftsman. His many interests called for management and supervisory skills and, sure enough, I was delegated to assist him in some areas of his work. There is no doubt whatever that his subtle thrust of responsibility on my youthful shoulders had a profound effect on my own later development as an entrepreneur. Rooted in my subconscious were thoughts of being of independent means, like my father.

He was also keen to see his sons with skills of their own as an anchor for the future. In my case I was sent for training in the shoe industry. Creatively turning leather into designer slippers and shoes brought to the surface a talent that flourished for a while and earned me some respect as a craftsman by all those who saw and wore my creations.

However, I soon developed a new interest in the island's public works department. My enthusiasm for work in public administration became the subject of many hours of lengthy discussions in our household.

This new ambition called for a course of study appropriate to employment in that field. My father was a great believer in being independent and would always be supportive of anything he considered could be gainfully productive. 'Ambition', he asserted, 'is the cornerstone of success.' He respected my wishes, approved my plans and agreed that I should go to England to pursue my objective.

The Trek from Morning Hill

What seemed a distant travel date was soon upon us. It was in stark contrast to the five minute walk from home to the local bus stop for the ride into Plymouth. This short walk somehow seemed to have lengthened by some tortuous calculation between distance and time which, no doubt, equalled an eagerness to get going.

At the bus stop, there was an extraordinary occurrence. In a matter of seconds, a sound like a fierce bolt of thunder vibrated around my head while a cluster of fireworks seemed to flicker in the distance. My heart pounded and a measure of unexplained joy filled my senses, touching the very depths of my soul. It was as if I was miraculously transported into another world of indescribable beauty suddenly, instantly, but all too briefly a nervous calm returned, leaving me wondering whether I was standing, sleeping or dreaming.

This experience, a hallucination perhaps, remains imprinted on my memory and somehow seems to have been the where and when of my journey into the wide unknown world.

The *Endeavour*, the bus that we took to Plymouth, was much later than usual and extraordinarily fully laden with sacks of sea-island cotton and other produce for market. It seemed as if there was going to be little room for my father, my sister Mavis, my suitcase and me in the bus.

After some rearrangement of sacks of cotton and produce, the conductor squeezed us in and we were on our way. I guessed the bus was overloaded, for she belched and groaned as she climbed Fogarty, the steepest of the hills on the way to Plymouth. At one point on the hill, *Endeavour* virtually stood still as the driver changed down into low gear.

Simultaneously, the conductor who was dangling on the back jumped off the bus with a wedge in each hand. He was obviously well drilled in placing the wedges behind the back wheels to prevent the bus rolling backwards before it engaged the bottom gear. This was a mind-blowing piece of manoeuvring that caused alarm. Fortunately, it worked and my fear of missing the boat lessened as we moved at a snail's pace into Plymouth.

The Italian Liner SS *Ascania* docked at the port of Plymouth, the island's capital at its predetermined time and date of arrival. Plymouth was a beautiful and quaint little town, which exuded a quiet, friendly dignity (before the volcanic devastation of 1997). Its architecture was picturesque and predominantly of Georgian influence, with buildings mainly of wood and stone.

The meandering road into Plymouth is a trail of sheer scenic beauty, a pathway through a cluster of rolling hills and verdant valleys all the way of differing shapes and sizes. Crossing Soldier Ghaut for the climb of Fogarty Hill literally takes your breath away. The road built into this hillside, engineered in a series of S-bends, viewed from Baker's Hill on the opposite side, is a picturesque work of art.

Climbing Fogarty, sufferers of vertigo are advised to keep well away from peering at the awesome precipice below. The scenery from the crest of the hill is a sure reward for the climb to the glorious views from the top—but not for long if you kept on moving—for this respite very quickly gives way to yet another steeply descending path into the village of St. Peter's and then slopes off into the flat of Woodlands, overlooked by the majestic mountains of Centre Hills.

Along the way, the drive takes you through Runaway Ghaut where, legend has it, if you drink from its refreshing mountain stream, you are sure to return for more. The route continues to wind its way through the beautiful village of Salem and descends into Belham Valley, an area covered with thick, lush vegetation where the wholesome smell of red cedar perfumes the air.

Prior to the fiery fury of the Soufriere Hills volcano, this valley was home to the island's golf course. The drive out of the valley delivers you to Cork Hill from where the road straightens out with views of the Groves Botanical Gardens, the famed Lovers' Lane, St. Anthony's Anglican Church and Sturge Park, the island's premier sports ground and stadium.

Clustered along Plymouth's narrow streets stood many offices, the hub and heart of the island's economy. Government headquarters, the courthouse, post office, hospital, police and all the other related services, the island's administrative pulse, were all to be found in close proximity to each other. In addition, the commercial and social sectors complementary to the delivery of a fully-rounded service left visitors lost in wonder at the remarkable efficiency of this small but not inconsequential island.

Leaving behind this paradise has been for most of her people one of their most difficult decisions. It certainly was for me. Apart from the island's many battles with Mother Nature (hurricanes and volcanoes), the decision to leave the island has always been driven by a search for education, employment and opportunity. The island remains a net exporter of its most valuable asset—its people. This situation has remained unchanged for generations and I myself have been part of that ongoing process.

There were many points of interest around the town. If you were to approach the pier on the corners where Bay and George streets meet, you could not fail to notice in the square that the war memorial enjoys pride of place. It is a fitting tribute to Montserratians who lost their lives in two world wars in the defence of the motherland. This monument, perhaps more than anything else, speaks volumes about the character of Montserratians and their loyalty to Britain, representing her contribution, however modest, to saving the world from fascist domination.

Amid parting tears and smiles, the moment of truth arrived as twenty-eight starry-eyed Montserratians prepared to board the *Ascania*, joining our regional cousins already on board from other English-speaking islands, all headed for the motherland.

Prior to my boarding the ship, three pretty girls sporting 'Mona Lisa' smiles paraded the pier with secrets each disclosed to me. They were not girl friends in the strict sense of the word, but I knew that each hoped she might be the lucky one to pin down my affections.

As a shy twenty-year-old reluctant to hurt the feelings of any admirer, my movements called for the skills of a gymnast as I worked my way through the crowds.

Eventually, I was cornered by Marcia whose eyes lighted up her face, signalling without words: 'I've got you cornered'. She proceeded to plant a daring kiss on my lips and at the same time slipped a letter into my hands and whispered in my ear that she could not resist the temptation of kissing me. It was, she remarked, a compulsion over which she had no control. Our conversation came to an abrupt end, for as luck would have it, a loud hailer sounded the boarding call for all passengers.

At precisely 4:15 p.m. on June 21, 1954, the liner lifted anchor and slid from her moorings. A rugged white foam-cushion followed in her wake, delighting the senses with its brief but fascinating play. At the same time, the waving throngs of relatives and friends on the pier, signalled their final farewell as far as the eyes could see as the ship headed west for England. The journey into the unknown was now at last a reality.

It was now time to read Marcia's *billet-doux*. Her opening lines made my heart beat faster for a minute: 'The sadness and loneliness I feel at your leaving' she complained, as if she was exclusively my woman. She went on: 'I love you dearly and will always be there for you. I do hope you will please write at your soonest with all the London news.'

Her actions on the pier, though perhaps well-meaning, had embarrassed me, and the tone of her letter inferred some kind of broken promise to which I was not party. So infuriated was I that, in a fit of madness, I released her letter into the sea and watched it disappear from view.

The new unaccustomed demands of life on water took some getting used to as the ship rode and rolled on mountainous waves, causing weak stomachs to give up their nourishment for the better part of 21 days at sea. Many travellers were confined to bed in the cabin or sick room.

Italian cooking, it appeared, did not cater to the taste buds of Caribbean folk, and together with the discomforts of being unable to keep down this unpalatable foreign food, weight loss and loudly grumbling bellies were very much in evidence.

Exploring permissible parts of the ship became an interest for me and it was during one of my interviews with the purser that I was made an offer of work to polish the brass railings. My curiosity and inquisitiveness must have impressed him.

It was quite a pleasant surprise after only a couple of days on board to find myself gainfully employed. This stroke of luck set me walking proud among my compatriots who were, for their part, gripped by jealousy at what seemed a coup so early in our journey.

The introduction to paid work was a confidence booster and made palatable my lingering fears of the unknown. It was a positive start which I knew my father would approve and be delighted to read of when the news reached him at the end of the journey. It represented in part his counselling. 'Make hay,' he would have said, 'while there is day.'

When not polishing brass, I found time for reflection and antici-pation--reflection on the things I missed most, relatives at the top of the list, followed by favourite foods. My imagination travelled back to the wafting smell of goat-water stew (a local Montserrat culinary delicacy) which usually excited my taste buds—the memory too of golden brown 'Johnnie cakes' that had the power to make me down them with a certain ravenous zeal.

The journey was the beginning of clear understanding, for the first time, of the meaning of a sheltered existence. In those moments of reflection, my father's dictum 'be smart' floated around in my head. It was impossible too, not to think of the competition for my attention between Marcia, Jane and Petra.

The Atlantic crossing had a profound effect on me as an experience of the world in which I live made fearsome at times by the vast expanse of the mighty ocean as I floated on it in a steel enclosure. It caused me to ponder in greater depth on the genius of man and his ability to roam and tame the universe. It caused me to think in a way I had not done before. In the quiet moments of solitary detention (as it were) on the high seas, I resolved to make myself more knowledgeable about the mastery of our planet and try to come to terms with my place in it.

Somehow, the days at sea seemed to grow longer, with weeks becoming months, and months seemingly years, until at last land was in sight. We had reached the Canary Islands. Cruising along its shoreline on a glorious, sunlit morning highlighted the impressive setting of the islands.

The imposing beauty of the landscape seen from the coastline thrilled my senses. A cluster of white-painted houses dotted the hillsides glistening in the sunlight among bottle-green trees. It was a sight that vividly recalled my wonderfully green Emerald Isle of Montserrat.

The liner moored at Tenerife for just a few hours and views from the deck of some streets and buildings appeared as if sanitised. It was a most impressive sight!

Our next port of call on the European mainland was the city of Barcelona on Spain's Costa del Sol. Setting foot on European soil for the first time made me feel a little like an explorer, causing a ripple of elation as my feet actually touched land.

The purser had made ready my pay packet which he handed to me as we docked. I thanked him with a firm handshake. The grin on my face must have stretched from ear to ear, for the purser chuckled at the sight of me.

It was certainly a moment to celebrate for there could not have been a better start to my prospects. A taste of paid work away from home was great stuff and the thought of spending it even more satisfying. For as it happened, this spell of employment earned me enough money to purchase my very first winter suit. A sharp grey herringbone tweed suit topped my shopping expedition in Spain. It was a purchase that filled me with a deep sense of pride and stirred up a new-found confidence in my ability to tackle whatever lay ahead. My good fortune at being offered work at the beginning of my journey was a good omen.

Our next stop would be destination Britain. What would the sons and daughters of Empire find, I wondered.

Encounters in a
New Land

As the *Ascania* steamed into Southampton, my mind focussed on what lay ahead. The farthest I had ventured in my twenty years was across the sea to the neighbouring island of Antigua, a mere twenty-seven miles, for one week with my grandmother.

The short trip was, however, to a large extent like still being at home and I had little difficulty in adjusting. Faces were familiar and there were only minor differences in the surroundings—a change of place that was easy to handle. England, on the other hand, would be my 'big adventure' and a world apart, as I kept telling myself.

What would I find? I kept wondering, as my history lessons kicked in. There would be Buckingham Palace, the home of Queen Elizabeth II and her plumed guards at the gates. It would also be interesting to see this London Bridge that was always 'falling down' as the song went, a favourite rhyme that children sang as they played on the island.

There would be Big Ben, reportedly the most famous clock in the world, the waxworks in the Hall of Fame at Madame Tussaud's and the sight of Lord Nelson's fall at the Battle of Trafalgar, all of which I had read about in school. It would be interesting to see Guy Fawkes with his gunpowder and wood, caught in the act of getting ready to blow up King James's men and the parliament.

Celebrating the capture of the Guy in Montserrat every November 5 was somehow part of a tradition that had filtered down to us in the colony. It would be interesting, I thought, to compare the glitz and glitter of the London fireworks with our poverty-stricken efforts in Montserrat. Celebrating the Guy for us meant a contrivance of old bicycle tyres cut into pieces and lit for processions through the villages. The oil-rich tyre content made for perfect flambeaus! How odd! And one might well remark, how come London's Guy became our Guy too?

The transfer from ship to train introduced an unfamiliar mode of travel and proved something of a hair-raising experience. This first leg of my travels went smoothly enough, adding to the journey a true sense of adventure as this amazing caterpillar-like machine of a train hurtled and puffed its way through hills, valleys and tunnels into London's King's Cross Station.

My first survival test was about to be put into action when out of the crowd a voice I recognised shouted my name as we moved along the gangway. Harold! Harold! it rang out. Not Anthony, not Tony, but Harold. What confusion, I thought, might well lie ahead with the use of names! Excited, I returned the unexpected greeting to the air around me, unable to contain the joy of bumping into someone from my village. This, I assured myself, was nothing other than providential.

It soon became clear that there were many others getting a similar welcome for earlier Caribbean emigrants had taken with them our island culture of care and made themselves available to offer advice and assistance to new arrivals.

The overall journey was, like an Alice in Wonderland tale, unfolding with each succeeding discovery as fascinating as the one before. Moving from ocean liner to train, from train to tube, from tube to bus, and on to our final temporary place of abode, all of which when added together, had quite a bewildering effect on me.

King's Cross Station stood out, with its quite stunning structure, as a hive of activity. The never-ending mass movement of people streaming in all directions conjured up the picture of a disturbed giant-sized ants' nest in motion. People seemed to be racing each other in all directions and, what was even more amazing, were not colliding with each other!

What a welcome to the capital of the world, I thought! This moment of bewilderment held me captive, mesmerised and unable to comprehend that there must be more people moving to and fro on this one station than there were in the whole of my island!

Our friend Fergus, who met us at the station, knew of the difficulty of finding lodgings and had organised for us to stay at a rooming house at 66, Southbury Road N4.

This temporary abode was something of a culture shock. My three friends, Kirnon, Lindsay, Molyneau and I were sorely depressed, We could not believe our eyes, dumbstruck that in a city where the streets were reportedly paved with gold, we should end up in a place like this!

It was a rude awakening to accept these facts of life yet not believing all the stories that had been put about. It was a tough lesson and merely the first of many such to be learnt about survival in a damp cold climate.

The room to be shared by the four of us measured approximately 16 x 16 feet with four single beds and little else. To be more exact, it was an involuntary camping house, to be survived and escaped from as soon as possible. The place should have been classified 'unfit for human habitation'. It was grossly over-tenanted; the rooms were dark and dingy, sparsely furnished and devoid of any dignity as a place of abode. When people spoke of 'culture shock', these were some of the situations that came to mind.

Our landlady was a plump, fierce looking woman with large piercing eyes. Her welcome was cold and coarse. The first item on her agenda was to settle the rent, payable one week in advance. Fortunately, we were prepared and settled as requested. And yet, as terrible as our circumstances were, we were forced for a time to endure a situation in which we had no choice. We were soon to discover what was behind the overcrowding. Notice boards in shop windows and press advertisements publicly carried the messages.

In most cases, these read 'No blacks, no Irish, no dogs and no children'. The more polite advertisements made no mention of the tenants they sought but, once on the doorsteps, you soon found out that if you were black, you were not welcome. It is difficult to describe the ordeal that most early emigrants faced in the search for a decent place to live.

Courageously, early black people battled this ugly and distasteful practice. But there was no alternative. Gradually, pooled savings through the 'partner system' were used to buy up some of the worst inner-city slums during the mid-fifties, early sixties and seventies. These precious purchases were painstakingly turned into somewhere we might proudly call home.

Black people's investment in the nation's housing stock runs into billions. Prime Minister Margaret Thatcher's great election promise of turning the UK into a property-owning democracy was already well in progress for thousands of emigrant black people subjected to the harsh racial realities of discrimination in the housing market. Those with a vision to invest in their own homes turned this adversity into a major advantage.

More than anything else, this strategic move demonstrates the hardy spirit of black enterprise at its very best. Many victims of racism thus driven with enthusiasm, were simply not prepared to allow the juggernaut of racism to ruin their precious lives.

It is estimated that some sixty per cent or more of the early emigrants invested their savings in brick and mortar and it will be interesting to see how this formidable hard-earned wealth will be used in the future.

The obvious next stage for black community development must of necessity be to seriously take on board the need to become part owners in the nation's economy. Active engagement in the process of wealth creation in all areas of national endeavour must take precedence if we are to claim our rightful place in the society in which we live and work.

Challenging discrimination in housing took several forms. Pooled private savings and voluntary self-help groups emerged to tackle some of the most acute community housing needs. Carib Housing Association, for example, founded in 1979 and chaired by Lee Samuel became a driving force in steering the charity and chalked up remarkable successes in dealing with some of the worst cases of need.

In 1983 dilapidated properties in Kensington and Chelsea were restored and named the Allan Kelly House after a distinguished community worker. In 1985 its second home, the Clive Lloyd House, was opened and named after the internationally acclaimed cricketer. Six years later, June 1991 saw the opening in Brixton of the Lee Samuel House, named for the association's founder, while in May the following year the Bishop Wilfred Wood House opened, named for the association's chairman.

This splendid effort influenced a trend that was to continue. Other housing associations followed, paving the way for a more enlightened policy both at local and national levels.

The Federation of Black Housing Organisations, founded in 1983 with the motto a 'Better Housing Deal', was to become another driving force in influencing change for the black community. The FBHO made good progress particularly in securing registrations with the Housing Corporation and has been instrumental in securing for its members greater participation in council housing management across the country.

At the end of the day, the all-important community lesson to emerge from our place on the housing ladder highlighted the need to take control wherever possible of our own solutions to problems as they arise. In the housing market it would be true to conclude that we brought about a civilizing effect in the provision of shelter, expanded the market, created opportunity and demonstrated without a doubt our creative abilities to avoid succumbing to adversity.

For emigrants, employment in the early days was plentiful, particularly in the poorly paid jobs that Europeans were not keen to do. Our good friend and neighbour, Fergus, who had received us as we alighted from the train, advised that we could walk into jobs the very next day at Lyons Corner House at Hyde Park Corner where he worked. We embraced the opportunity with enthusiasm.

Directions on how to get there were detailed in every respect. Bus number 4 took us to Hyde Park Corner and back. Lyons Corner House was minutes away from where we alighted from the bus and, as luck would have it, getting to and from work was made easy, as the bus was routed directly past where we lived.

We found the place without much difficulty, were interviewed and were asked to start work the next day. It was evident that they were anxious to get us into the kitchen as quickly as possible and did everything to speed up the process.

But on the first morning we were to set out for work, our island culture surfaced. It was raining! We complained to our landlady that we could not go to work in the rain. 'You are all mad!' she exclaimed. 'Rain does not stop anyone from going to work here!' And with that chastisement we were off and away, quickly dropping that Caribbean habit.

We duly arrived at work and were promptly initiated into the art of loading and unloading crockery on and off the kitchen conveyor belts that serviced the dishwashing machines—a monotonous and soul-destroying exercise—but we were happy all the same to be employed.

The reward for this first foray into the world of work in Britain was £4.80 per week with breakfast, lunch and dinner thrown in for good measure, and I would concede that the servings of kippers for breakfast were outstandingly delicious. Apart from being boring (pun intended), the work bore no relation to my ambitions. It was, however, a means to an end and accepted as such. 'The Adventures of an Economic Migrant' had begun to take root.

Work in the kitchen was without a doubt a major learning curve to what the real world was about. In any case it helped to install and cement the all-important bricks of self-awareness, assertiveness and the need to take seriously one's personal responsibility for life's journey. My father's dictum 'Be smart' was never far from my thoughts.

As I recall, the return journey home from work that first night turned out to be quite an eventful experience. Alighting from the bus at the right stop went smoothly enough, but finding where we lived was a different matter altogether for at night everything seemed extraordinarily different. In short, we lost our way.

The unending rows of look-alike terraced houses with poor lighting made it extremely difficult to identify our home that first night. To make it even worse, our house was on a square where the same number popped up three times. After circling the block several times, Lindsay and I, purely by guesswork, rang a bell and got it right!

Kirnon and Molyneaux, our two colleagues, arguing that it was the wrong house, kept on walking only to be brought home next morning by the police! Rescued by the police, they had slept at the station. This was a chilling experience, but provided a good laugh as we relived the experience with others in the next few days.

All journeys have one thing in common. The traveller can never predict life's terrain with any certainty nor be sure where its path will lead. Experience has taught me that faith in one's abilities and being at all times focussed can make the journey less burdensome.

My arrival during summer in the midst of the unaccustomed long daylight hours, made me examine why at 7:00, 8:00 and 9:00 p.m. there was still bright daylight. Was this London on the same planet as the one I came from? Nothing could have prepared me for the fascination of the changing seasons as they revealed themselves.

On the heels of summer, the changing face of the days that led to autumn breezed in with equal captivation; elegant trees soon became scenes of golden brown and set about shedding their leaves. Leaves that had once been green pigments of matter now fluttered and floated gently down to carpet the earth in readiness for yet another stage of the cycle of things. Such scenes were, for me, delightfully riveting.

Yet the true initiation into the arms of the motherland was still to be experienced. Winter—bitter winter—was the season for which I was ill prepared. My tropical lightweight clothing offered no protection from the damp, piercing cold that numbed my senses and made my teeth chatter uncontrollably, leaving me unable to stand still at times, turning my every breath to a kind of smoking chimney.

The cold was misery—a misery far worse than the bites mosquitoes or bedbugs could inflict. My escape back to my homeland was an ever-present contemplation. Wearing thermal underwear, long johns and the rest, made a difference. Sensitivity, however, to these new unfamiliar garments gave rise to a skin irritation that left me always wanting to scratch. This condition, alongside the suffering from chilblain-reddened toes and fingers, caused me to wonder: Was this some kind of penance?

In an effort to escape the dreadful living conditions of our over-tenanted house, I explored as a priority the possibility of buying a house of my own. It was patently clear to me that the money paid out in rent could easily cover the mortgage for a house. This ambition was realized in 1957, in joint ownership with my sister and her husband, three years after arriving in the UK.

The Bible teaching that 'by the sweat of thy brow thou shall eat bread' was well rooted and remained a guiding principle in my approach to work in the kitchen. Every experience, I reasoned, represented an opportunity, and one that I must use to settle in, build a cash resource, get familiar with the geography of the city and the employment landscape, readying myself for my next move at the right moment.

Predictably, as I found my way around the city and the job market, choices emerged that were significantly more rewarding than the Lyons Corner House, but I was keenly appreciative of my first adventure. With more satisfactory living accommodation and improved conditions of employment at Commercial Radiators, an engineering company in Tottenham, I was now strategically placed to pursue my original objective. I enrolled at the College of North East London for a course that would lead to qualifications in public administration.

Among the subjects studied was English Literature which I found immensely enjoyable and rewarding. It led directly to the discovery of a talent for creatively recording my observations of the handling processes of converting steel into an indispensable item used every day in every home—the cooking stove. The result was the personification of steel in this poem I wrote.

29

Silent Steel

Within the green covered case,
Lying in her bed of oil and grease
Silent Steel's smiling face
Expressed the joys of restful peace.
They took her from her cosy bed,
Tween guillotine placed her head,
Still silent—smiling though in pain,
No words of moaning or complain',
Pieces many made they of her,
All shapes and sizes sunder,
Notches and folds all relevant,
On and on this process went.
Sweet shapes! Full pleasing to the eye,
A steadfast gaze doth satisfy,
Fair Steel in beauty dressed!
Still smiling, and still at rest.

Time spent at Commercial Radiators was not only more financially rewarding, but was also a relaxed and creative period in my life. Other pieces of work followed, some of which are to be found in other writings.

It was a period that saw the emergence of leadership qualities shaped by the workplace. Working conditions in the factory left much to be desired and I found myself being invited by the workforce to be the spokesperson about many of our concerns.

On arrival for work one Monday morning we found the factory frozen cold. All the heating systems were switched off and action had to be taken to restore them. It was agreed that we lay down our tools and go on strike, although we were not unionised.

The foreman, who was our first line of authority, showed no interest in our complaints and carried on with his work. The general manager, on his arrival, was most upset to see us not working and started swearing at us.

It was the moment for me to assert the 'spokesperson' status conferred on me by my workmates. When the manager had finished, I calmly asked him to let the managing director know that I wanted to speak with him, and he did. Failure on the manager's part to do so, would have given me a known right of the workforce to speak directly to the MD about anything we were unhappy about.

The assignment as spokesperson was to test my negotiating skills in my meeting with Mr Wilkinson, the managing director. His office was some five hundred yards across the road in another building. As I entered his comfortable office, he greeted me warmly. 'Come on in', he gestured. There was a glowing coal fire burning brightly in his room. 'How can I help?' he enquired. I smiled and commented on his fire before answering his question. 'Are you aware, sir,' I asked, 'that there is no heating in the factory?' 'But it is cold', he retorted and, excusing himself, picked up the telephone. Having ended his call, he thanked me for coming to see him. 'Go back to your work,' he ordered.

On my return to the factory, I found a hero's welcome. The heating had by then been restored. Improved working conditions and respect for the workforce flowed from that meeting like never before. It was my practice run for a leadership role.

On the whole, the company was good at dealing with its employees. In my case, I was released one day a week to attend college although my studies would not directly benefit the company. I am truly grateful for what was a major turning point in my career development. The time had however come for my next move and Commercial Radiators was a useful staging post on my journey.

A personal audit at this juncture pointed to three milestones that made a difference: there was a home that was my own as long as I paid my mortgage and work was enjoyable and fulfilling with my stated long-term objective very much in the frame.

In the meantime, my interest in the voluntary sector to which I was always attracted had become a passion and led to membership of several organizations. First of these was the Finsbury Park Methodist Church International Fellowship, which I was instrumental in launching with like-minded friends. I was elected its Chairman, with my good friend the Reverend Kingsley Halden as Secretary. The organization became a springboard for community leadership in other areas that were to emerge later.

Gravitating to the church was as natural as eating, given my upbringing and background. This move was a link that admirably bridged the gap in areas with glaring cultural differences. A good example was the use of the church hall for community social events. These events filled a void in the expression of Caribbean culture as against the more reserved nature of British culture. The joviality of Caribbean events soon had us all loosening up and regaining some part of our fun-loving selves.

However, one difficulty was finding a way of confining the natural exuberance of our members in a residential area. I found leadership and tact to be the key essentials in making things work in the best interest of both communities. I became an active member and later was invited to become society steward in the church, through which role I was in a position to influence change.

A study of the history of Finsbury Park was a most interesting subject. It was a place filled with fascinating stories that carried all the hallmarks of the playground of the aristocracy of earlier times. The huge homes overlooking the park together with others on Queen's Drive and King's Crescent bore witness to a more extravagant past. As London expanded, the area became home to thousands of people of emigrant stock of a more transient disposition.

When I became a member of the church, people of the Caribbean diaspora represented a mere five per cent of the congregation. Today it is quite the reverse. People of African and Caribbean origin now represent the majority of the congregation.

There has also been transformation in the nationality of the church's witness during the latter part of the twentieth century. Its ministry has continued through difficult times, but remained constant and resilient in proclaiming the Gospel, with black-led churches showing the fastest growth.

There were other notable community groups with whom I connected in the late fifties and early sixties: the North London West Indian Association, the Montserrat Overseas People's Progressive Alliance, (which sounds like a political party but is not) and the West Indian Standing Conference in which I served as Housing Officer. These groups and others were the engine for emigrant welfare and resettlement and a catalyst for change.

Community fieldwork has led me to believe that emigrants, of whatever creed or colour, coming into a new society will always be faced with a number of handicaps—some real, others perceived. In some cases, it may be the language, the level of certain skills and the need to conform or adapt to local norms and behavioural patterns, all of which may in some ways lead to prejudice of one kind or another.

Prejudice against people because of colour, affects an individual in two specific ways. The first is what I call a kindly contemptuous tolerance; the second, and more extreme case, is abusive rejection. The majority of emigrants have in many cases lived and experienced one or other of these situations, but often use each difficulty to strengthen their resolve to correct, as far as possible, these unfortunate situations. This has been my preferred way of tackling racism.

The noble objectives of all the groups with whom I have connected have been driven by nothing other than the longing to foster good and harmonious relations, which one hopes will, in the future, lead to a more just and equitable society.

After living for many years in London, it remains my view that change is continuously taking place, perhaps a little more slowly than most decent people would like to see, but, thank heavens, it is happening.

Group expertise in solving many social problems has, to a large extent, cured much of the divisive inter-island tendencies that have played havoc among Caribbean people in Britain. The big island/ small island divide was a major source of friction between folk of poor intelligence or narrow minds—or both. This shameful behaviour still persists, but to a much lesser degree.

One of the most frequent causes of friction resides with the white press and their failure to correctly identify the perpetrators of the crime. Too often all black crimes were (and still are) labelled Jamaican before the facts were established. Both police and journalists have too readily rushed to conclusions.

Some tangible benefits were to flow from active group work, among them the building of a culture of trust in the popular 'partner system' which allowed its members access to a large pool of money used in many instances to finance deposits on homes, motor vehicles and other substantial purchases, which might otherwise have been out of reach.

The big gain, however, for inter-island groups, has been the ability to speak with one voice, uniting and integrating the islands into what might be called a 'regional constituency' of the Caribbean in Britain—a constituency significantly larger than many of the English-speaking islands.

Within this constituency there are big stakes to play for. I believe that, in time, by cultivating and building on our common heritage, we will see the emergence of tremendous economic benefit flows and skills transfers into the Caribbean region of the twenty first century. For Britain there remains a large pool of labour and skills to draw on, to say nothing of the huge trading benefits that would continue to flow between ethnic British-based businesses and the emerging markets of the region.

The growth in inter-island marriages has already made for a healthy integration process with major spin-offs for the region in a number of ways. First, there is organic growth in the tourism sector, laying the foundations of connecting with our roots across the diaspora. A climate of investment inducement will further help to expand the regional economy. A big plus is that our climate lends itself to being the place most people would like to work and live, given improvement in employment opportunities.

There is no secret that the Caribbean constituency in Britain has over the years amassed a huge pot of wealth that remains untapped. I believe ways must be found to encourage and secure investment routes for the transfer of some of this wealth into the region. This is a matter for serious consideration by Caribbean governments and businesses. As people and a region, we have much to offer, and exploiting our many assets has to be at the top of our agenda.

The highly developed Credit Union movement in some of the islands (particularly Jamaica) is but a short distance away from achieving its full potential in line with the mega-prosperous, Co-operative Stores Operations in the UK, the nation's largest business. It is without doubt that a model for Credit Unions in the Caribbean. With effort similar to that invested in CARIFESTA, the region's festival of culture and arts, all things are possible.

Two and a half decades ago my family and I attended CARIFESTA hosted by Barbados. Once more I came to the conclusion that the people of the Caribbean, like no other region of the world, radiate a special charm, warmth and hospitality that could do much for creating unity in a world divided by bigotry.

'I have a dream of literature inspired by the peculiar temperament of West Indians, paintings inspired by the tropical jungles of Guyana and the beautiful waters of the Caribbean', so said the late Forbes Burnham, President of Guyana. Most people, I am sure, will readily concur with those sentiments.

As I arrived with my children at the Grantley Adams International Airport, the spirit of the region captivated me. Broad, beaming smiles and laughter lighted the faces of everyone in sight, while drums and pipes poured out a warm melodic welcome.

That Barbados is internationally well-known for its hospitality was—instantly obvious. The pageantry and precision of the presentation at the opening of the festival will forever live in the hearts of all those who had the good fortune of participating in it.

The National Stadium stood ablaze with colour against the background of the harmonious hum of the 300-voice inter-island school choir. The ceremony honoured men and women for their outstanding contribution to the culture and heritage of the region and will forever remain a cultural landmark in our history.

It was an extraordinary explosion of folk songs and calypso; free verse and prose; paintings in oils and watercolour—an enchanted spell! As Wordsworth said of a sublime occasion of his: 'Bliss was it in that dawn to be alive... But to be young was very heaven!'

The Enterprise Mantle

Moving into employment that matched with my original goal was a key factor in determining what would happen next. On reaching the intermediate stage of a course in accountancy and brimming with confidence, I applied for a position in that field through the Brook Street Employment Agency in Wood Green, London. They found me a placement with the Smart Weston group of companies in the accounts department of their head office at 3 Eden Grove, London N7.

This assignment was to test fully and put into practice what I had learned in the accountancy classroom. My new boss, Finance Director Louis Segal, was a man with a presence, bristling with immense energy and wearing a permanent smile of contentment with his life. He drove a 'Rolls' and shopped at Harrods, both symbols of taste befitting a man of his standing.

His company owned over two hundred menswear stores all over the UK, and my first task was to reconcile the gross takings of these stores and have the weekly figures on his desk by midday every Monday. Louis impressed on me the importance of this task, especially its demand for accuracy. He also pointed out that, as far as he was concerned, the cash balances on the company's books were the most important tools in managing the whole organisation.

The wisdom implicit in his statement remained fixed in my mind and I was later to appreciate fully, the intricate implication of the cash book balances as the key tool in the science of management.

Entrusted with what, after all, was a major responsibility, I naturally gave the task my best shot, and recall my great sense of satisfaction when the postings of the cash were reconciled to the penny, meeting to boot my demanding deadline. I struck a chord in my boss's good books.

Meeting deadlines and targets greatly impressed my employers; quick to recognise potential in me, they accordingly promoted me with an improved salary package and still greater responsibility within the organisation.

The additional role that landed on my desk was the implementation and monitoring of the debtors' listing, incorporating a credit control function. This area of work required secretarial support with authority to delegate. It was in essence a most useful training exercise in hands-on administrative management and communication skills which would become indispensable in events that were to unfold later in my career.

Under Louis Segal's tutoring, it soon became clear to me that I was destined to go into business on my own account. He was my inspiration.

One of the great lessons I learned on this leg of my journey was that nothing equalled putting theory into practice and gaining priceless operational experience along the way.

The experience gained at Smart Weston was invaluable as I made my first foray into the world of business on my own account. While still working for the group, I launched Carib Services, a trading company to test a business formula I labelled the CS Purchasing System. This unique concept was intended to show how it was possible for a business to improve its bottom line at no extra cost to the company.

Selective mail shots to test-market my ideas were successfully introduced and I gained the confidence to give up my safe bread-and-butter job for the challenge of the market place.

Louis Segal recognised my entrepreneurial qualities, intimated that I could make it on my own if ever I wanted to, and that he would not stand in my way. This seal of approval from one of the brightest men in the business gave me the courage to launch out on my own.

Most people go into business with the profit motive in mind. A small number of idealists want to help their fellow men. I entered business to achieve economic independence. I cannot claim that I was always confident, but one thing is sure, I was always an optimist.

All along the way, I encountered many of the problems faced by aspiring new business people as I sought to build solid foundations. Some problems were specific to people of colour, and like thousands of immigrants, I had lived through this kind of perversity, which would be laughable were it not so hurtful and destructive.

But, I resolved very early that I was not going to be held back or be obstructed by such idiocy. Often have I used these same contemptible antics to my advantage, certainly in terms of developing the mental and moral toughness indispensable in dealing with racists.

Having seen hundreds of my people driven to the edge of despair by this mindless cruelty, I was determined not to be a victim. Fortunately, I have the temperament of a poker player, though I am not one. I rarely betray emotion; I work hard to stay in control and hardly ever flap. I also anticipate some of this imbecility so that I can checkmate the perpetrators. This exercise can, at times, be tedious and time-consuming, but I philosophically took them in my stride.

Sometimes, I must confess, I derived great pleasure from humiliating some of the morons who tried to make my life miserable. In the end, I had one powerful weapon on my side: that as a buyer of products and services, I had a wide choice of clients, some of whom recognised reluctantly that money has no colour.

Celebrating at the Miss Dyke & Dryden Ball

Left to right: Mr Dudley Dryden, Mrs Daphne Wade,
Anthony Wade, Mrs Agatha Dryden, Mr Len Dryden and friends.

Community Development

I made no secret of my commitment to the struggle for equal community rights and the need to be actively engaged. It was my passion and I became actively involved with issues that called for improving the lot of our people in a number of ways. Membership of pressure groups that worked for equal opportunity was central to my thinking and, to that end, I was relentless in pursuing any activity that would lead to a more equitable society.

Through my community and charitable work, I had built up an impressive circle of friends and acquaintances across the city. Some of these friends felt indebted to me for some small act of kindness or helpful advice that flowed from the work I did and I could count on them for support of my ideas.

Then in my twenties, I was at the age often referred to as that of the eligible bachelor and, as it happened, most of my close friends were women. The truth was, however, that the door to my heart remained firmly closed to a serious relationship for the time being.

This reluctance somehow seemed to add to the wad of Valentine cards that came my way each February, the envy of many of my mates who were lucky to have even one. The cards created an awareness of my vulnerability and made me always keenly mindful of that danger, so that I avoided close female encounters that could so easily lead to situations that I might well regret.

At the same time, strongly believing in the estate of marriage, I was not averse to entering into holy wedlock with 'Miss Right' at some point in time. For the moment though, there was the other heavy matter of a career at the top of my agenda. This calculated decision was a maturing experience, aimed at preparing me for manhood.

But as they say, reward sweetens labour and the achievements at Smart Weston had the effect of bolstering my confidence, not only by being more productive within the company itself, but also by opening up offers and invitations to assume key leadership roles within the community which would in time prove useful.

The experience gained and its subsequent transfer to benefit the community filled me with a deep sense of pride and I was set to transform my whole world and fulfil my ambition to be a man of independent means.

Involvement in community social affairs provided a platform to spread the merits of disciplined hard work. It also kindled the awareness of self-worth and a belief that discipline in all things must underscore community pride in itself. Believing in this core value, I seized the opportunity to emphasise it at a community Valentine dinner at which I was the guest speaker. Discipline in all things I contended was the basis of success, whatever the task and a much-needed area of focus for community progress. These were my closing remarks: 'Dedicated discipline has been and remains a simple success formula and, routinely applied to any task, always ensures success for the individual and the group.'

The speech was received with rousing applause and a standing ovation. It was a confidence-building moment for me and in a way, served as my leadership initiation within the community. There was no question about their agreement with the views I had expressed.

The response overwhelmed me. Shouts of 'Ride on, brother! Ride on' echoed across the room. The audience loved it. And the community would remain the judge about that leadership role they had imposed on me that night.

At my table that night, sat a stunningly beautiful, buxom Jamaican nurse. She was particularly vocal on the big/small island debate taking place at our table. This issue had dogged and divided the Caribbean community for years. She was a very intelligent woman and she knew that I hailed from one of the small islands.

It appeared as if I might be the butt of some of her ribbing. Throughout I remained calm, parrying each of her verbal missiles with a mild and indulgent smile. I guessed she must have had some ulterior motive, or possibly wanted to test my reactions and tolerance. This was the only rational conclusion I could come to, and yet it seemed at variance with the standing ovation I had just received, of which she had been a part. I consoled myself with the knowledge that in all things you win some hearts and lose some, and this must evidently be the case here.

She seemed everything that a man could desire in a woman: attractive, vivacious, educated and endowed with all the graces of a perfect lady. She was the toast of the men around her. They simply adored her and I was no exception, but could find no opening for declaring my admiration. The firmness of her small-island attack allowed me no courage to even hint at how I felt about her. Her performance that night earned her the nickname 'Lady Ribber'.

Several months later, bumping into each other at a club member's home, we exchanged pleasantries. I was in great form and boldly addressed her as Lady Ribber. She was greatly amused and laughed so heartily that tears ran down her cheeks.

A game of scrabble was about to begin and I could barely disguise my delight at being invited to participate, not only because it was a game that I loved, but also because it would give me time with Lady Ribber. She volunteered to do the scoring, which meant writing out the four players names in full. A flash of concealed delight privately stirred my emotions at being in her company again.

As fate would have it, I got a beating. For my pains, I collected the scoring sheet as a trophy to mark the event and asked all the players to autograph the document, making it worthy of being framed. They all commiserated with me over the beating and I left with my trophy feeling positively good about it all.

Certain social events in the community depended largely on organisations' membership lists for informing the community of special events. Invitations to these events came from a cross-section of society, embassies, high commissions, government bodies, charitable groups and others.

It was for one such special event that an invitation arrived from the First High Commissioner for the West Indies, British Guiana and British Honduras requesting the pleasure of the company of Mr and Mrs Anthony Wade to a celebration to mark Federation Day for the West Indies.

The invitation, an RSVP affair, caused me to be slightly perplexed, as there was no Mrs Wade or even a girl friend, despite my many good friends. Yet I wanted to attend to be part of this historic moment which meant something to me.

Lost for a solution to this pending puzzle, I sought the advice of my good friend Peter who, without hesitation, suggested that I invite Lady Ribber. This I did through her sister and was over the moon on learning that she had graciously accepted to be my guest.

I duly communicated the outcome to Peter who was also unattached and more daring than I. He immediately volunteered another great suggestion, to be my chauffeur for the occasion using his brand new Triumph Herald for the ride to the reception at the Connaught Rooms in central London.

This was all quite unbelievable, considering how she had publicly tried to humiliate me because of my small-island origin. I had however, during the dinner debate, slipped in some punches of my own, asserting that small-island men make great husbands, and insisting that she please take note of that fact.

Furthermore, I had commented that a book was not to be judged by its cover, or an island by its size, drawing as an example the size of Britain compared to its immense wealth and power against huge land masses of parts of the world that were poor and unproductive!

It was going to be interesting to see what emerged from our date.

'From 'Boyhood' to 'Manhood' to 'Fatherhood'

In Love for the First Time

The evening had finally arrived. Peter was a no-nonsense timekeeper and arrived spot on time for the drive ten miles away to collect Lady Ribber from her sister's home.

As we neared the house, the tension started to build. Not a date, merely an escort for an occasion, I mused. This whole thing is quite weird. She will pose as my wife, I kept on reminding myself what the invitation quite clearly stated '...requests the pleasure of the company of Mr and Mrs Wade...' 'The announcement, Peter', I spluttered nervously. 'What announcement?' Peter enquired. 'The Master of Ceremonies will broadcast the names as we are presented to His Excellency and mine will be a brazen lie I could hardly ever live down!' 'Come on man, don't be a chicken', said Peter. 'Get in there and enjoy the fun, and remember to sneak me in if ever you can'. 'Of course, I will do my best', I said, not much calmed.

The MC was no doubt from the top echelons of the Toast Masters' Guild. He was regimentally attired and somehow seemed to have smelled an impostor being tagged along on my arm. His announcement of the arrival of Mr and Mrs Wade rang out in a way that appeared as if the microphone had suddenly gained in volume so that the sound bounced back and forth across the room for all and sundry to hear.

The greeting from His Excellency and his Lady, however, was of such warmth that my terror soon vanished. With the formalities out of the way, it was now time to explore the informal admittance of Peter, which fortunately went without a hitch. With that accomplished, my return journey home was now also taken care of.

As expected, I was met and greeted with a barrage of questions from acquaintances I had not seen for some time. This was a well kept secret, they all tuned in. When did it happen? And why had they not been invited? This episode certainly caused an exceptional stir and set tongues wagging for there were no answers to their questions; no agreeing nor denying.

There was finally a window of opportunity for me to enjoy the company of my escort. She wore a gorgeous blue gown that dazzled with accessories designed to both complement and accentuate her personality. But how did Peter fare?

He landed happily into a hurricane-style romance that changed the course of his life that night. A beautiful, petite and professionally accomplished concert pianist living in London engaged him in conversation for the entire evening. On parting that night, she whispered to my escort and myself 'I like your friend and we will meet and talk again soon'. That said, she drifted off with her cousin, a first secretary at one of the High Commissions.

Having no such encouragement from my escort, I dutifully returned her to her sister's home, thanked her for gracing the evening and assured her that her company had provided the most enjoyable evening I had ever had, for which speech I was rewarded with a peck on the cheek that met with my enduring satisfaction.

I was absolutely delighted and savoured my peck as though it were a permanent patch on my face, remaining intoxicated for days by the charms of my escort. Whether I had scored any points with her was a question to which I had no answer. I therefore resolved not to be too pushy but to give myself time before my next move.

Among my Valentine card collection, there was one that had made a deep impression on me and thinking about it was never far away from my thoughts. Can the words of this love-arrow that pierced my heart be real, or were they just a jester's prank? The guessing and the intrigue numbed my senses. I think I must have read the love lines a thousand times or more. Their haunting call read:

'Thinking of YOU on VALENTINE'S DAY—If I knew your love was mine, dear, could I call you just my own, I would taste far deeper gladness than I have ever known; And my dearest wish, as always, is just to be near you. So please dear, be my Valentine, and make my dreams come true.'

The sentiments expressed in the card sank into the very depths of my soul, evoking the following response to this anonymous admirer to which I penned an answer by way of a sonnet entitled, 'To My Love'.

I had a go at playing detective. The handwriting on my Valentine card somewhat resembled that on my scrabble souvenir sheet but to be sure it had still to be confirmed and a solution to the guessing found to reveal from whence the secret arrow came. As the weeks went by, the thoughts of the mystery card gnawed at my very soul.

Could it possibly be Lady Ribber? I wondered. I most certainly would be overjoyed if it was but how to find out remained the billion-dollar question. One possibility, I thought, might be to invite her out for a meal. At our parting I had said how much I had enjoyed her company and she might well be expecting to hear from me again.

Courageously I acted upon my intuition and extended an invitation to her to be my guest for dinner. Two weeks later there was still no response and I was almost a nervous wreck. The pain of waiting for an answer was becoming unbearable. I was virtually her prisoner. Could she possibly know?

A third week had almost winged away and I was by then doubting my sanity when her letter came cheerfully accepting my invitation. I was over the moon, and thrilled to bits by her acceptance. The trick now had to be how to handle this second date. The selection of an appropriate place to dine was paramount.

I settled for a candle-lit dinner at the Savoy and hoped the choice would convey my taste for the finer things of life, and in particular, my feelings about her. I hoped for a window of opportunity in handling the delicate matter of finding out if my Valentine card came from her.

The setting was wonderfully relaxing. As we finished the meal, I fished out of my breast pocket what I referred to as 'my most prized possession'. At the sight of the card recognition flooded her face. Ah! She gasped with immense relief that the game was at last up. Her smile changed to a radiant glow, an expression of great joy...her arms reached out in a fond embrace and her lips did the talking... 'I love you' I whispered slowly, waiting for the words to sink in before placing my hand-written sonnet 'For my Love' in her hands for her to read.

Speak up! my heart and tell
Ease your pains; being chains
'Tis not enough alone to dwell
Way upon love's gold-paved plains.

Speak up! my heart and tell
Of love, each breath is sweet,
No mortal tongue can tell,

Where love's sweet soothing symphonies meet.

Alas! Enough that I can say,
My heart dances to the music,
Rejoices at the birth of each new day,
Feels the power of love's magic.

Speak up! my heart and tell
Let my lover also know it well!

An ocean of emotion engulfed us both. The release of our shared feelings in those moments instantly struck a chord. The dreams she had dreamed of the man of her choosing and my dreams of my 'Miss Right' instantly became a reality and plunged us into a furnace of love.

As she read the verse, tears of joy trickled down her face, followed by sobs of happiness. This was what she had hoped for and dreamt about, she exclaimed. 'Here you are, my very own prince,' she sighed, 'my own true Valentine.' And 'You my darling,' I assured her, 'will always be my Valentine.' 'You, my darling,' I continued, 'are the inspiration that gave birth to this sonnet. You will note in the octave, that my heart took flight and soared to "love's' gold-paved plains" and got lost in its alliteration, to "sweet soothing symphonies". In conclusion, it "cried out to speak up and tell, and let my lover know it well."'

'But what if my card had not arrived, would you have found me?' she asked. 'It was you my precious darling' I replied, 'who held the keys to my heart. Now you have opened the door and stepped right in where you belong.'

Her big, beautiful brown eyes flashed a signal of happiness and her luscious lips reached for mine. Lovingly I stroked her hair and surprised her by disclosing details of my many attempts to claim her attention.

She pinched my ear lobes with both hands and admitted that she had seen my body language a few times but reminded me that she was still a student then and, with the broadest smile of satisfaction, explained how she had prioritised the pursuit of her career before setting about to find her man.

We marvelled at the circumstances that had brought us together and agreed on its divine ordination. It was love at first sight, unplanned and unhurried, taking its course in a manner to which questions would provide no answers, even if we tried. That night sealed a guiding principle for our journeying. Sharing we pledged in its totality—sharing in everything inspired a song I dedicated to her that night.

Of everything that's dear to me—near to me
Close to my heart, you are a part
Of everything I think about or care about
My sweetest thought—your loving heart

Refrain:
You are the sweetest flower of early spring
Crowned with beauty and adorable.
Sweet as the pearls of early dew
Shining as the morning sun peeps through.
Dearest to my heart—are the joys we impart—in everything.

Of everything that's bliss to me- this to me
Lives in my heart for evermore
Of everything that I possess—your caress
Here's happiness for evermore.
(For refrain see Appendix 2)

I recalled my teenage conversations with other boys as we chatted in the moonlight in Montserrat, often letting our fantasies roam wild. My soul mate, I had sworn, would be a nurse and sure enough, my teenage dream had come to pass. The woman of my dreams had successfully completed her first objective of attaining her professional ambitions and now had within her grasp the second—to marry the man of her dreams.

Instantly, love's treasure chest revealed to us like never before its hidden secrets—the thing we both had longed for—the fun of planning and doing things together. Theatre-land was among the places we frequented regularly for the best of what it had to offer: plays, musicals and concerts, not forgetting the ballrooms where we danced and where love blossomed.

While it was clear that we shared the same dream, I was struggling with accountancy at evening classes and holding down a job. My soul-mate was keen for me to complete my studies and sought ways of helping. Mindful of how she had managed her own studies, her idea was to take a short nursing contract in Trinidad for two years, so as not to be on hand to distract me. Furthermore, time away, she concluded, would certainly test to the full our faith in each other and the strength of our relationship.

Her proposed sabbatical abroad speeded up our engagement after eighteen months of courtship. With little fuss and few frills, I decorated her ring finger with an exquisite diamond of her choosing. All that was left now for me to do was to wish her Godspeed and to promise to press on with my own career.

The reaction to our engagement from her relatives was one of non-approval that their sister had become involved with a small-island man and they did not hesitate to let their views be known.

She was strong-willed, knew her own mind and was insistent that at the age of 24 she would not be lectured by her relatives on how to conduct her love life. She was furious and assured me that their objection in her view was secondary. She was sure of herself, and for my part at 27 I knew that I would never let her down.

A Testing Time

As she prepared to depart for the land of the hummingbird, she transfixed a penetrating gaze into my eyes and in dulcet tones whispered, 'I am travelling for love—your love'. At a loss for words, I asked her to say that again. And she did. She held my hands, kissed my forehead and repeated: 'Travelling for love, for love of you. Just you wait and see.'

From that phrase, I penned and dedicated to her yet another song— 'Say that again.'

Say that again—I love you
Say that again--I'll be true
Darling and when—when I'm not with you
I hear the echo of I love you

Love is a song two hearts must sing
Love is the world's most wonderful thing
Even at night, all the world seems bright
From the moment that you whispered, 'I love you'

Say that again—I love you
Say that again—I'll be true
Darling and when—when I'm not with you
I hear the echo of I love you

All of my life was empty and blue
Hoping and praying a dream would come true
You called my name—set this heart aflame
From the moment you whispered, 'I love you'

Say that again--I love you
Say that again—I'll be true
Darling and when—when I'm not with you
I hear the echo of I love you
(music sheets in Appendix 2)

In response to this song she wrote, 'I found comfort in the words of the song and still hear the echo of "I love you" vibrating in my head as though it were there to stay.'

Independent of mind and confident of the correctness of her decision to give me space to get on with my studies, she cheerfully said her goodbyes and moved quickly through passport control and the departure lounge for travel to the land of steel band and calypso.

In our last few moments together, she handed me a sealed envelope, inscribed in bold type, 'please do not open till I am out of sight'. This act filled me with apprehension and gave me the jitters.

My spirited confidence was for a while dented as I pondered what the contents of the envelope could possibly be. My imagination ran riot and it took me hours to summon up the courage to open the envelope. I held my breath as I eventually opened it. There was no holding back a burst of instant laughter as my eyes lighted on the first lines:

My Darling Prince, you need to know that last night I did not sleep. I cried the whole night through at the thought of leaving you behind. I questioned myself over and over about the wisdom of my decision although it was taken with your agreement. I prayed for divine direction and must exercise faith in the decision I made.

Yet, somehow I feel a little afraid about your vulnerability to the competition I've left behind. You may well question this less than confident tone of worry. Well—some of my so-called girl friends who you know, told me to my face that once I was out of sight you would become a target. I know, darling, that you can take care of yourself. However, I hope you don't mind me revealing this to you.

I don't mean to question your love for me, for I know in my heart just how much I mean to you. I put this feeling down to the tension of leaving, especially now that I will not be physically near to hug and hold you as I have grown accustomed to do. But I assure you that you are in my thoughts every moment. All my love.

From her nurses' home in the sunshine, she was soon to become a prolific letter writer. Her tally of the written word was enormous, and ran into several letters a week.

Messages From Across the Sea

'There is an internal tug-of-war going on inside me, between you and my contract, and it is the hurt that I feel that is driving me crazy. I can tell you from now, that it is my intention to break my contract. It will simply be a question of timing.

Settling into my new environment stresses me out to the point where I considered catching the next plane back home. I am physically in one place and mentally in another, and constantly going over my not so smart reason after all for this self-imposed exile and unnecessary heartaches.'

She had however, among her many gifts, a personality that charmed and correspondingly had the knack of building friendships easily. It was not long before her new colleagues warmed to her. They dubbed her CDS, an acronym using the first letters of her name and adding their own interpretation to it, which for them stood for Cute Darling Sister. She was immensely touched by this act of friendship; it made her feel really welcome.

CDS was a sharp, crisp and endearing form of address. She loved it and reminded herself that her middle name was my favourite. As if by magic, my letter arrived then conveying her birthday greeting using her name to format the greeting.

Birthday Greetings Sweetheart Daphne

Today—always, you are my sweetest thought--
Everything I think about, or care about, is your loving heart,
Tis why, today I choose to say
D is for DARLING the best there could be
A for AFFECTION so pure and so free
P brings PERFECTION which makes
H means HEAVEN forever blessed

N says you're NOBLEST among all the rest
E for ETERNAL inscribed on my heart
That's what DAPHNE meant right from the start
So here is all my LOVE in greetings
And all the JOYS this birthday brings
I share with you—SWEETHEART
Happy Birthday!

She wrote that the card took her breath away and left her wishing she had wings to fly home. Her sobs of joy filtered outwards into the room next to hers attracting the attention of colleagues who hurried to her only to find her overcome with emotion by the intensity of the love my birthday card conveyed.

The reaction of her colleagues upon reading the card was hardly predictable, but their female instincts somehow led them to weep with her. Having cried together, they laughed together at the fun of it all. As flying into the arms of her beloved was not an option, the next day she penned the following letter:

'My birthday card is something I will treasure forever. It is much more than a mere card—it is an inspired literary outburst that speaks from the depths of one soul to another. It has lit a flame that will live forever within me. Darling, being stuck in this place is a punishment I have foolishly inflicted on myself with your blessing, and I am now paying the price for it. I hang on to every kiss at the end of your letters. But oh, how I long for the real thing! Your darling ever.'

One of her many letters came registered in a curiously wrapped little bundle that had to be signed for. I eagerly ripped open the package to find a second layer of gold wrapping paper. Whatever could it be? Reduced to a state of nervousness, I removed the gold wrapper that revealed a tin of Yardley's talcum for men.

I was thankful for my talcum and pleasantly moved and surprised at the effort she had put into sending this gift. But I looked at the tin again and again. There must be something more to it, I thought, perhaps some special properties. What could it be?

The key to the puzzle soon came to light in a letter that arrived some days later. In the text in bold type were the words OPEN THE TIN AND SEE WHAT YOU FIND. Still suitably mystified I carefully prised open the tin and emptied its contents onto a paper napkin on the table. Having carefully sifted through the delicately perfumed powder, to my great delight, I found a glowing object of precious metal staring me in the face. A band of gold!

This was a complete knockout. It took me time to recover from the beautiful suspense and surprise of it all! Regaining my composure, I carefully examined my treasure. On its inner circle were engraved my initials. I popped it on my finger and marvelled at the exact fit. Her next letter was music to my ears.

'You will be delighted to hear that I have given my notice and am breaking my contract, as I said I would. There may well be some difficulty, but whatever it takes, I am getting out of here as soon as I can. I miss you too much and can bear it no longer.

I cannot live without you anymore. Wanting to bear your children is what I want more than anything else in this world. My heart aches for you more and more each day. Why did I leave in the first place? I will never know.

I am happy in my work delivering other women's babies, but the more I carry on, the more anxious I get about settling down with you and having babies of my own. Two little girls for me to dress up, and a boy in your image for you to take with you to cricket and football! I hope that's fine with you? I still cannot fully understand why I am out here.'

In fulfilling a second boyhood goal, I had already taken the step of buying a home for my wife-to-be rather than sharing the home I already owned with my sister and her husband. I duly communicated the good news to her that I had secured for us a home of our own. She was well pleased.

A date for the nuptials was mutually agreed and I was mandated to look for a church with good aisle spacing for her approval. I dutifully agreed.

By then, she had informed her relatives of her intentions and tagged on at the end of her letter what amounted to an ultimatum. 'In the matter of my marrying the man I love, it is either that you are with me or you are not, it is up to you to choose.' She knew that her sisters, despite their protests, would hardly go against her wishes and would stand right beside her. And they did. The countdown was now on.

Reunited

She could barely contain herself in physically connecting again. There was lots to talk about and plenty to do before the June 16, 1962 the agreed date for our wedding.

Methodical in her approach to whatever she did, she had already prioritised the order in which she would start after running them past me. The place we would call home came first on her agenda, followed by a visit to the church she had asked me to look at.

After inspecting the house at 39 Napier Road N17, she was intoxicated with happiness. Her big brown eyes sparkled, signalling her total satisfaction with the place she would make into the cosiest home there ever was.

The long-awaited event finally arrived and her sisters, despite their earlier professed disapproval of the union, pitched in and ensured that their little sister's big day went smoothly. In fact, they very much regretted their earlier objection. Not so her brother, the most outspoken against her marrying a small-island man. He stood by his objection, refusing to attend the wedding.

With the ceremony now behind us, it was time to escape and claim for ourselves some peace and quiet away from the dictates of others, to start living our lives the way we wanted to.

I had done my level best to pick a place that was specially created for lovers. Nothing was left to chance. That I was overwhelmed by the warmth of the reception we received on our arrival at Cowes would be to understate the grandeur of it all. Every feature of our cottage was crafted in love and positively designed for the removal of any lingering inhibition on the part of new couples. The setting creatively succeeded in freeing the human form as nature intended it to.

My wife, for her part, had meticulously sourced a honeymoon kit of some of the finest and most sensually-charged lingerie items she could lay her hands on and could hardly wait to see my face when I beheld the fine silks and laces she had acquired for my pleasure.

Celebrating our togetherness called for sharing a toast to the fulfilment of our dreams that love would have its way. It was now time to recapture some of the many events that brought us together. We sealed our good fortune with a fond embrace, and our affections for each other found its natural expression.

She recalled, and disclosed for the first time, how she had heard from girl friends on the boyfriend-hunting circuit, how they had coined me in 'Mr Man' language as 'Mr Neat & Tidy'. They confided to her that they had all had eyes on me but found it extremely difficult to engage me in light-hearted conversation. Putting it bluntly, they said 'I had a way of shutting people out', which was off-putting in trying to get close to me. 'In a manner of speaking, it was as though you had a bolt on your heart, and I am glad that I was the one to unlock it', she revealed. We both roared with laughter till the tears ran down our cheeks.

She reminded me of the time we were introduced at her sister's home of the polite, but rather matter-of-fact 'How do you do?' I gave her and then simply dismissed her. It was nevertheless in those very moments, she said, that she had fallen helplessly in love with me.

She also disclosed how she had discreetly carried out her own due diligence on me prior to posting the love arrow I had so aptly spoken about in my letter. We agreed we were lucky to be a Valentine couple.

It was time also to reveal that sitting at my table for the Valentine dinner that night was carefully arranged once she knew that I was going to be there. She then confirmed that the ribbing I got was to test how well I would stand up to what she knew would be thrown at me by her relatives and wanted to see how tolerant I would be in dealing with what, after all, was a view held only by bigots. Of course, I had passed her test with flying colours.

These heart-to-heart conversations gave me the chance to bare my soul about the mental struggle taking place in me in a choice between my accounting studies and a business career. My gut feeling was to give free reign to the spirit of enterprise that had taken me over. I produced my plan B for our security in the event the business did not work out as I intended. 'I trust your judgement, darling', my wife assured me, thus giving my plans her blessings.

But those blessings did not include her political beliefs, an area in which we were dead opposites. She was a staunch Labour supporter and admired Labour's philosophy on state ownership, while I held Conservative views on private ownership. She was a staunch admirer of Prime Minister Harold Wilson. She admired his pipe smoking and tried to have me smoke a pipe, for she thought it a pretty hip thing to do. She even bought me a pipe at Cowes, complete with tobacco and accessories. Against my better judgement but in an effort to please, I had a sporting go at the pipe for a while, (without tobacco, I might add) but was forced to give it up on finding that the stress of gripping the pipe between my teeth made them hurt.

Cowes was a fun place, known not only for hosting the world's most famous yachting races, the Americas Cup, the Admiral's Cup, the Cowes Power Boat Weekend and countless other yachting events. It is also a well-kept secret paradise for honeymooning couples to let their hair down away from prying crowds. Apart from sailing, other leisurely sporting activities that filled our days included horse riding, rambling and softball cricket.

A softball game of cricket on the island is one that I wished I had never volunteered for on that holiday. As the only West Indian male on either of the two teams I found myself in great demand for they assumed that every West Indian was a cricketing star. I failed dismally—bowled out first ball for nought! My wife felt the pain of defeat for her hero so badly that she disappeared instantly and was found later in the bedroom with a pillow covering her face at the disgrace I had brought upon her!

Notwithstanding this major humiliation, the irritation soon passed. Our escape to the island was otherwise a rapturous, restful and propitious start for us as man and wife.

'Honey' was a term of endearment she bestowed on me from time to time and it reminded me that the words 'honey' and 'bee' belonged together. As the song goes about love and marriage, you can't have one without the other. This inspired a new song dedicated to her.

Honey Bee

Oh! Oh! Oh! you honey bee
Whatever in the world have you done to me?
The stings you gave me keep itching me
Oh! Oh! Oh! you honey bee
You're an angel from above--you're surrounded by my love
In my heart you've got a room--our love will always bloom
I love you so much I don't know why
Don't think of leaving, you'll make me cry

Take my heart take the key
Oh! Oh! Oh! you honey bee

Oh! Oh! Oh! you honey bee
Just what happens when you kiss me
You thrill me so much in all do
All my loving is just for you
(music at Appendix 2)

Our family life became the talk and envy of many of our friends. Some marvelled at the way we operated, as if we were programmed, and wondered if our formula was capable of being packaged, so that they might copy our marriage model. Daphne laughed heartily at the suggestion and referred them to her song 'Everything', reminding them with characteristic wit that her husband had written it and that we lived by it. Marriage meant sharing, she explained, in the simple things of life, underwritten by mutual love and respect, the only secrets on which our union was built.

The simple things of life, she continued, quoting from Emily Matthews, are:

...the keys to happiness belong to everyone on earth
To recognize them as treasures of great worth
The changing of the seasons, the rising of the sun
Moonlit nights, restful hours on a lazy afternoon
The relaxation of the mind in laughter, the beauty found in truth
The wrinkled eyes of wisdom, the innocence of youth
Dreams the heart has woven, letting go of cares
And countless answered prayers
Loving bonds of family ties, and understanding friends
The chance to make a difference, the will to make amends
Having some one's hand to hold, the promise each day brings
The keys to happiness are found in simple things.

Her lady friends marvelled at the ease with which she rattled off the recipe for our lifestyle, but what, they insisted, were the steps for finding 'Mr Right?' Intelligence gathering, she explained, was the trick. Once you have spotted your prince, be your own detective and research the finer details about him: check out all you can about him, his character, his habits, his friends. This undercover work required getting the process down to a fine art, she declared. Again, her friends all gasped at her thoroughness and thanked her for the superb lesson.

We had pencilled in our provisional travel plans, to try and see as many parts of the world as we could before children arrived, although she secretly hoped that she would get pregnant on our honeymoon.

In any event, considering the part the celebration of the federation of West Indies had played in bringing us together, we decided that our first choice of places to visit must be some of the islands.

Jamaica and Montserrat topped our 'to-visit list', for they were the islands from which we hailed. During our travels, one thing emerged, commonplace and distinctly pronounced. It was the friendliness of the people of both islands, the compelling spell of enchantment that pervades the region and guarantees instant relaxation as you touch these shores.

Everywhere we travelled the sound of music filled the air. Villages and towns alike were alive with a warmth and energy that made our hearts flicker with delight and our feet tap to the music.

On her first visit to Monteserrat she could not avoid noticing the many similarities to Jamaica. She loved it and dubbed it 'Jamaica in miniature'. Both islands' flora and fauna were much the same. Montserrat's verdant rolling hills and mountains were equally picturesque. The gentle Caribbean breeze that caressed the land, combined with the friendliness of its people, captivated her completely.

We were proud that we belonged to a region known the world over as the 'relaxation capital of the world' and were pleased to be doing our bit towards integrating it.

She continued to pursue her career as a midwife and looked forward to the day when she too would become a mother. She recalled her girlhood fantasies, a career first, a husband next and a family. Four years after we were married, she became worried about her failure to conceive.

Her restlessness led to investigations and infertility treatments that eventually brought about the happy event for which she longed. On July 7, 1966 at 5:20 a.m. a precious little baby girl weighing eight pounds came into the world to fulfil our dreams.

She insisted I be present at the birth, and I dutifully obeyed and held her hand and shared in the mystery and agony of her labour. I would not have had it any other way. There was great rejoicing at the arrival and she named her Deborah Anne (Anne in honour of my mother). The day I became a dad was the happiest day of my life.

I left my wife's bedside at 7:20 that morning feeling ten feet tall and went out to spread the good news to our relatives and friends, the proudest man in the world as I strode into our local florist's to collect a huge bunch of roses for my wife.

On my return to the hospital later that morning I was led to the Sister's office and greeted with the news that there was a temporary setback in my wife's condition. My heart missed a beat. It took some consoling to calm me down, as Sister explained the complexities of post-natal depression. They advised that I should not be unduly worried by this common condition that usually soon passes.

Despite their assurances, I was still visibly shaken but did my level best to force a smile as I entered the room with my bunch of roses. She smiled back at me, but it was a vacant, tired smile. As I held her hands lovingly she remained distant and listless.

Back in the Sister's office I sought her assurance and was again comforted by her assurances. Yet I returned to the ward with a heavy heart, kissed my wife and prayed that normality would soon return. It did after a few days.

A proud mother and little Deborah Anne arrived home to a rousing welcome and lots of fussing over her from everyone, relatives, friends and neighbours who joined in the celebration. She was soon her old self again and directed all the arrangements for baby Anne's comfort. In the meantime I regained my self-confidence and told my wife that something had miraculously happened that I had never thought possible.

She was all ears and prompted me. 'Come on Daddy, out with it!' she demanded. As someone not usually lost for words I found it difficult to explain. 'Darling', I stuttered, 'after that beautiful experience, my respect and love for you have increased a thousand fold'. I embraced her and she understood.

'We are now both grown up!' I declared, 'obedient to the good Book—"be fruitful, multiply and replenish the earth", Genesis 2:28.' I must admit that I was somewhat nervous learning to handle my cute baby daughter to begin with, but soon mastered the new art. Sharing in everything was the key plank on which our relationship was built and reaffirmed and, to that end, I insisted that I would be my baby daughter's night nurse. My wife smiled and agreed that we had a deal.

Tony Wade Junior arrived six years later, so named by his mother in my honour. His arrival had proved even more difficult for his mother than his sister had, but with the same happy ending. Our cup of joy overflowed, fulfilling our dreams.

In keeping the faith, there was always the guiding principle to which we had committed during courtship, continuing to share in everything. I savoured every moment that I could, sharing in meal times, bath time and story time. I lived that commitment and enjoyed it to the full. Home was a place called 'Happiness' and while it was tough blending it with the exacting demands of my business life, I always found a way to spend quality time with my family.

There is no way one can truly understand the joys and fulfilment of sharing in everything until you experience together simple things like changing nappies, getting the bottle ready for the baby, getting up at nights to attend to its needs and to be a helpful all-rounder in the home. This is the stuff of which real life is made and it is a blessed privilege to share in it.

Among the priorities that we had set ourselves was providing our children with the opportunities we ourselves had not had at the start and, to that end, the children's education programming started in the crib. My wife's child-care training and her own grounding prepared her well to pursue her children's preparatory lessons with comfortable ease. No effort was to be spared in making sure that our children had a good education as a mix of both private and public schools was selected.

Moving up the residential ladder where the better schools were to be found was a prerequisite in achieving this objective. We moved home from Tottenham to Woodgreen where Deborah Anne was born but were unhappy with the local schools and opted for private schooling for her in Muswell Hill some distance away.

Crescent Road where we next moved to, had seen better days, but was certainly a better neighbourhood than Tottenham. We quickly set about renovating the house making it much more pleasant to live in. Our elderly English neighbours were full of praise for what we had done but let slip that it 'showed them up'. I offered to give their home a facelift at no cost. They were overwhelmed by my generosity. Ours is a friendship that has endured.

By the time Junior arrived we had moved again to Queen Elizabeth's Drive in Southgate, a more desirable neighbourhood where the local schools were excellent. He moved through the grades and on to university where he majored in philosophy.

Deborah on the other hand had from an early age decided that the career route she wanted to follow was to go to drama school and we encouraged her to do so. She had choices and opted for a place in dramatic arts in Pasadena, California. To her credit she excelled in her chosen field.

The notion that one's education is not complete unless one is reasonably well travelled sits well with my way of thinking. Drawing on my own experience reinforced my views and broadened my understanding of the world, and it was something I wanted my family to share. Exposure to the world outside home and school, 'the look and learn formula' I called it, was the ideal complement to one's education.

Unlike at Woodgreen, our neighbours in Southgate were somewhat toffee-nosed and rather aloof. On the day I arrived at the house in one of my company's vans, my new neighbour was standing in his drive. I greeted him warmly and he returned my greeting, asking if I was the painter. When I said I was the new owner, his face registered surprise. I smiled at his body language and he saw my amusement. It was an awkward moment for him and he apologised profusely. I accepted his regrets and offered him the hand of friendship.

This house too was in a poor state of disrepair. In fact it was the shabbiest on the street, but by the time I had finished the make-over, it had become the most desirable. Yet our new home was somewhat unsettling. It was plagued with a strange constant smell of fish, especially at nights. The smell persisted although no fish was cooked in the house. Because it was most pronounced in my daughter's bedroom, the smell frightened her so that she would scream at nights and run into our bedroom. This strange pattern of events was brought to the attention of our minister, the Reverend Fred Clifford, who successfully exorcised what must have been a spirit with no resting place.

In much the same way we traded up homes, the time came to trade up the family car. Being a reasonably practical man, affordability and economy always figured in my acquisitions. Starting with a nimble Ford Anglia, other workhorses to follow were a Morris 40, a Hillman Minx, Hillman Hunter and Rovers. As our finances improved, a prized Daimler and a Jaguar would fill my ultimate ambition. These purchases afforded us enormous pleasure, especially in exploring places of interest across the country. Motoring holidays in Wales hold fond memories of the fun we shared in Bognor, Anglesy and Colwyn Bay.

During a planned family holiday in Jamaica during Christmas 1978, a serious illness surfaced for my darling wife that was unfortunately wrongly diagnosed.

Earlier that year a routine examination of her breasts showed up a lump. Following the regular procedure a biopsy was done to determine the nature of the lump. The results came back declaring the lump to be non-malignant.

While in Jamaica, she began to experience excruciating pains as never before and we hastily returned to London for investigations. As it turned out, the result of her biopsy had been wrong. With no explanation of how such a careless error might have occurred, it robbed her family of a wife and mother.

Throughout her pain and suffering, her strong faith and belief in life after death saw her through. As she sailed through the valley of death she had no fear, finding comfort in the knowledge that she was safely in the hands of her heavenly Father. People who came to visit her in hospital marvelled at finding themselves the ones to receive words of comfort. She shouldered her cross with the dignity by which she had lived and expired at the relatively young age of 42 on January 9, 1979, to rest in peace with a smile on her face in the company of angels.

The loss of her love and affection as wife and mother left a marked aching gap in the household. Her colleagues at work and patients alike remember her cheerful and fantastically infectious, caring personality.

Her life remains a testimony of faith and hope felt not only by her immediate family, but also by all who knew her and often sought her valued personal counselling.

In memory of a wonderful wife, I registered The Daphne Wade Cancer Trust with the Charities Aid Foundation for research and the detection of cancer. The deed stipulated that the proceeds of the Trust were to be shared equally between Imperial Research Cancer Fund, London and the Jamaica Cancer Society—a request dutifully carried out. After this the fund was closed.

Her final words to me were: 'Life goes on so continue to live as a man'. What a practical woman my wife was!

My faith sustained me through those difficult times as did the prayers and support of my relatives and my brothers and sisters in Christ, enabling me to take into my stride the adjustment to her loss. I now became all things to my children.

With the passing of a loved one, only a firm faith and trust in the divine plans of the Almighty can heal the broken-hearted. Comfort and strength are to be found in Paul's words in Second Corinthians 12:9. 'And he said unto me, My grace is sufficient for thee: for my strength is made perfect in weakness. Most gladly therefore will I rather glory in my infirmities, that the power of Christ may rest upon me.'

In December of the same year, the children and I were looking forward to settling down to our first Christmas without Daphne when a near fatal accident threatened to shatter our lives. I left a student friend at home with the children while I went shopping for toys and returned home an hour later to find the house in complete darkness.

I was greeted by my neighbours with the horror story that there had been a fire and that my son was in the burns and intensive care unit at Chase Farm Hospital in Enfield. From there he was transferred to the Northwood Specialist Burns Hospital where he spent 45 days. It was a harrowing experience but, thank God, he survived to tell the tale.

The circumstances surrounding the accident remain difficult to understand. He was clever at making Welsh rabbit (toasted cheese sandwich) on the top shelf of the gas oven, by himself but under supervision. That day it seems that as he lit the oven, escaping gas exploded in his face. He had the presence of mind to cover his face with his hands protecting his eyes nose and lips, but his clothing was set alight.

He got down under the kitchen table and rolled screaming so alerting his sister and a student friend who were in an upstairs bedroom. They called a neighbour who was able to brave the fire and smoke and drag him to safety. We remain forever in the debt of that good neighbour.

The physicians did a fine job of repairing his forehead, face and hands with skin grafts from his legs. Back at school, it was unbelievable the cruelty he had to endure with the names he was called by other kids: 'Burnt toast', 'Scar-face' and others too terrible to mention. Tolerance is a virtue, a lesson he had taken seriously. To his credit he was able to withstand his tormentors and take the ordeal in his stride.

I am eternally indebted to the following friends and neighbours: Priscilla Duberry who took care of my home and my children during my many journeys aboard. Pearl Goodridge who managed my office, Kelly Henry, a family friend who claimed Junior as her son and provided after-school care and Jill and Ann Coles on our road who took care of the daily morning school runs. They were all pillars of strength.

This chapter in my journey speaks profoundly of the joys of life and our frailty and suffering. It tells me that we must give thanks to the Almighty in all things and at all times.

Building an
Industry

The building of an industry usually takes a generation, and in each generation there are pioneers. I have often been referred to as belonging to that very select band of people.

A partnership of Dyke & Dryden was founded in 1965. Its core business was selling pre-release records. Two and a half years later the partnership was dissolved and a new company, Dyke & Dryden Ltd succeeded the partnership with my acquisition on June 12, 1968 of 33 per cent of the equity.

This chapter looks back at the steps that were taken in what was to become a major turning point in my journey: my employment at the Smart Weston group of companies, was for me a milestone. It saw my move to a totally new career change; it saw the emergence of the entrepreneur in me fighting to emerge. At this juncture, I gave up my relatively comfortable bread-and-butter job for the independence of the market place as I started a trading company, Carib Services.

There is no doubt that this was a daring step that took some guts. The move triggered a change in my personal journey and had an impact on the lives of many people as will become clear as the story unfolds.

Networking organisations, the platform for information gathering and the exchange of ideas, is an invaluable forum for business people. It was at such a forum that I disclosed to my two friends, Len Dyke and Dudley Dryden, who were already in business, that I had given up paid employment for the challenge of a business career. They wished me well even as they disclosed the difficulties they were facing in their own business.

My commercial experience at my old job was common knowledge to them and they asked whether I would care to look at what they were doing for a basis on which to join them in their enterprise.

Four weeks after giving due consideration to their proposal, I was clear in my own mind about what I could bring to the table which I believed would change the course events at the business. I agreed to their proposal, placed my own Carib Services on the back burner, and threw in my lot with them as soon as the paper work was in place.

June 12, 1968 ushered in a new corporate structure with a share capital of £100,000. This bold new beginning was to transform the company's operations with far-reaching ramifications in a multitude of ways for the black community in Britain.

Although there was a change in the structure and ownership, there was little to indicate that change had taken place. The trading name remained the same and the paper changes were not in the public arena.

My new colleagues suggested a company name change to Dyke Dryden & Wade Ltd. I felt this was not necessary—an error of judgement on my part which was later to prove detrimental in many respects.

Initially, some customers wanted only to deal with my colleagues whose names appeared on the fascia board, when in fact, the person they really needed to speak to was me. In the interest of good public relations, I found it always necessary to spend time explaining how a body corporate operated.

Unfortunately, distrust runs deep in our community and remains a major handicap when financial resources are pooled. This can so easily become a hindrance to the all-important financial building blocks used so effectively by other ethnic groups.

Advisors, acting for the old partnership, solicitors and accountants, were retained to draw up the new agreement. The accountants, on the basis of their working knowledge of the business, dismissed the proposition of my investment in the company out of hand. They deemed it not viable and advised me against entering into the new venture.

It was with a sense of gutsy delight that I took a firm stand with the accountants, explaining that while I respected their professional views, I had to insist that they too must respect my desire to invest my hard-earned cash as I chose. I laid it straight on the line. My instructions were to be followed since I paid their fees.

There was obviously something I knew that they were not party to, and it was this knowledge that formed the basis of my willingness to invest. I knew that there was a huge demand within the black community for black hair and skin beauty products and I saw the opportunity of taking advantage of the gap that existed in the market.

I was confident about what I could bring to the business, provided my colleagues were willing to allow me a free hand. To their credit they did, and allowed me full administrative control of the day-to-day operations of the company.

With the agreement signed and sealed, it was now up to me to demonstrate my ability to turn the business around. Achieving that goal was not long in coming and I must confess to immense pleasure at the sweet smell of success as I delivered what I promised.

Our accountants asserted that my views were flawed and gave the impression that they alone knew what was best for the company, even being disparaging in a most contemptuous manner.

My dealings with them demonstrated that if one's faith in one's ability is strong enough, an individual can challenge and conquer whatever goal he/she sets him or herself and success becomes the reward for personal self-esteem. Here was the spirit of the entrepreneur within me at work.

The stand I took and the subsequent proof that their assumptions were wrong finally earned me their respect. From then on, my views were always taken seriously. Hard work and determination, combined with the courage of my convictions were the key ingredients in the delivery of good, positive results. The company grew and became a force to be reckoned with. The accountants were fired for poor performance!

As the chief administrative officer, it was up to me to set the company's operating parameters, the goals to be met and the standards by which we had to work to attain them. I subscribed to the old school of thinking, that leading from the front was the only way and being hands on was paramount. I recalled some wisdom I had picked up about leadership earlier on, and applied what was a simple doctrine.

> 'The boss drives his men; the leader inspires them. The boss depends on authority; the leader depends on goodwill. The boss evokes fear; the leader radiates love. The boss says "I"; the leader says "WE". The boss shows who is wrong; the leader shows what is wrong. The boss knows how it is done; the leader shows how it is done. The boss demands respect; the leader commands respect. Be a leader, never a boss!'

I applied this principle throughout and found that, philosophically, it was simplicity itself, and a novel road to relationship management within the organisation. It gave ownership to the team by making them responsible for their actions and their performance.

Speed was of the essence if we were to reverse our losses. My overall administrative responsibility allowed me the freedom to move quickly in whatever direction I considered to be in the best interest of the business. The most pressing task at the time requiring immediate action was a review of the current state of affairs and the preparation of a plan for the way forward.

Love of music is an innate part of the Caribbean cultural heritage and is part of our baggage wherever we travel. It was natural, therefore, for the pulsating rhythms of sun and sea to accompany the many travellers to places outside our region.

Sound System Kings, the party-music providers of the sixties, played an invaluable role in the social life of the community in those early days. Music from home kindled the fun-loving spirit of the islands and made house-parties a popular feature of black social life that helped to brighten the dull, dark days of winter.

Important as the music was, however, my first strategic move was to take the company out of the music industry. You may ask why? I would answer that although the record business was a good one, my colleagues did not understand it, nor did I. What I immediately understood was that records stacked on shelves, covered in dust, could not be given away, let alone sold. On the other hand, with hair preparations and cosmetics, stock that did not sell one day would sell the next. It was that simple.

Closing down the records side of the business was a small price to pay to save the company from certain bankruptcy. This move was cause for great rejoicing by 'the sisters'. They had found a store that now catered to their beauty needs. The store at 43 West Green Road, London N15 carried a refreshing choice of hair and skin preparations and won their endorsement. They flocked through its doors in droves and spread the good news.

Unmet demands for products to satisfy the special needs of thousands of black women were not carried by established businesses and spotting this gap in the market was a timely move. Spearheading this development meant that the company over the years became synonymous with the industry and created a humming hive of activity that impacted on the business and community life in a number of ways.

Building an Industry

The phenomenal rise of the company ignited an explosion in an enterprise culture that energised the black community as never before. The company produced good economic results and involved the community. Early benefits included family 'fun-days' in Epping Forest and the very popular event, the 'Miss Dyke & Dryden Beauty Pageant', held once a year at some of the finest hotels in town, became a date in the diaries of the upwardly mobile.

Sponsorships of fashion, motor racing, and a number of educational activities were among the prized community activities supported and promoted by the company. On the education front, black pupils were singled out and placed in educationally subnormal schools (ESN). The company viewed this development seriously and became the prime backer in providing the campaign funds to have the schools closed. This was money well spent and an outcome of which we were justly proud.

Identifying the gap in the market and doing something about it was a visionary manoeuvre. It shaped the company's growth pattern in an organic manner. Retailing became the cornerstone of the business to a point where wholesale distribution and exporting departments had to be created to meet the demand nationally and overseas. Product development and manufacturing were next in line and led to the vertical integration of the organisation.

The impact of a black-owned company finding a solution to some of our community needs was not lost on some of its members. Getting involved commercially soon became a model to follow and, accordingly, new black-owned businesses started springing up all over.

The community spirit of enterprise effectively came alive. It accentuated the positive and was an education in self-help that provided for the creation of skills and employment. It drove home, like never before, the importance of wealth creation and signalled a community confidence that we were as good as anyone else.

Penetrating the market through existing white-owned stores was something of a major battle. Racial discrimination and ignorance played a devastating role in forcing customers to travel long distances to purchase their products. Innovative ways had to be found to get white stores to carry our products. A first step was to organise a number of black customers to call into their local chemist stores, ask for the products and inform the proprietors where stocks might be had. This strategy worked and gained us limited acceptance.

A second and far more effective approach was to hire white sales staff to call on existing white-owned stores to stock our products. This strategy was far more effective and forced their competition to follow, which made a difference with new entries coming into our segment of the market and expanding it.

This exercise, as I recall, gave rise to a number of laughable incidents. There were times when some white customers wanted to see the boss either to negotiate quantity discounts or for some other matter. It was always amusing to see the look on their faces when my white sales people introduced me. It was an unbelievable insight into the misguided perception of many white clients that a black person could not be the boss.

The final stamp on the industry came about with the founding of Afro Hair & Beauty Ltd. It became the marketing arm which promoted the industry across all its various segments. It brought diverse businesses together from many parts of the world under one roof in London each year at Alexandra Palace—an event aptly referred to as 'the shop window of the industry'.

A strategic company policy to assist and encourage new young black businesses was to offer free-stand space each year at the Afro Hair & Beauty Exhibition. This start-up opportunity to give exposure to new entrants was greatly welcomed by those fortunate enough to get stands.

While there have been several persons to benefit from this policy, one good example of a start–up was Treasured Moments, a florist who got her business up and running by being selected to provide the floral service to the exhibition. The company became a star performer.

Dyke & Dryden and its subsidiary Afro Hair & Beauty prospered and made black social history by becoming the largest black-owned businesses in Britain in the last quarter of the twentieth century.

Of major significance in this whole scenario was the pioneering and entrepreneurial spirit kindled by the breakthrough. It released a latent source of energy and confidence within the community, demonstrating that, with commitment and hard work, all things are possible.

This achievement engendered a vibrant 'can do' spirit with both companies becoming household names and a reference point for progress, defying racism and some of the many barriers that stood in the way of black progress. The message was unmistakable and clear.

We did it; so can you. It was an inspirational lesson soon to be copied by others.

On the education front and of equal importance, was that this initial success provided opportunities for some students writing their thesis in business administration to use Dyke & Dryden as their company of choice as a case study in the industry.

Two questions asked by every student who interviewed me stand out. What was the secret of your success? What was your unique selling formula? There were no simple answers I would explain, but typically my comments would indicate the qualities needed among them: a clear objective of what you would like to achieve; a sense of purpose; and, a will to succeed. One should be unflappable and have the ability to tackle several things at once. If the interviewee showed an interest in what I had to say and was willing to carry on, I would normally consider him/her serious about the mission.

One such person was Mr Eric Osei, who interviewed me in November 1993 for his Masters in Business Administration. It was gratifying to hear from Mr Osei who wrote some months later as follows: 'Please find enclosed the profile I did on you for my MBA assignment. I got a distinction for this piece of work'. He went on to express his delight at having been able to complete his studies through a business within his community.

Another case in point was that of Mr Francis Okwesa. Francis was at Strathclyde University preparing for a marketing degree, and also attended for an interview to complete his thesis. Our discussions went well; he thanked me and went off full of confidence to complete his studies. Some months later, impressed by what he had heard and seen, he applied for the position of Sales and Marketing Manager with the company. He was successful and became a key player and an outstandingly resourceful member of the management team, serving the company well and leading in the development and promotion of the company's own brands programme.

The success formula for the company had several components to it. In the first place, its operations struck a chord in meeting a community need in the marketplace, by filling a gap overlooked by established businesses in the general market. Its success became synonymous with the aspirations of a neglected community to break out of the den of despair in which we found ourselves. Members within the community shared that dream and were intricately involved, making the business in many ways a community company.

Further, the company took its corporate responsibility seriously and built a special kind of relationship with its clients, mindful of its own painful beginnings and providing community support wherever it was possible to do so.

Team building was perhaps my most successful achievement in gathering around me people who shared my vision. This was an absolute necessity, carried out with the help of the persons named below.

Joan Theodora Sam became my first secretary. She was fiercely ambitious and fitted nicely into my way of thinking. I very quickly discovered that, while her salary was not great, she was more concerned about learning as much as she could and looked to the future rather than to the present. Her steadfastness and loyal support paid off handsomely for both of us for, by the time she was ready to take the plunge into business on her own account, I was there to offer her my hundred per cent support in her endeavours.

Pearl Goodridge (already mentioned) who succeeded Joan Sam and was an able and strategic cog in my management wheel, a first-class all-rounder. She filled two key roles, as Executive Secretary and as Personnel Manager. She came on board at the time of the company's fastest growth. She became my eyes and ears, was efficient, honest and dependable and freed me from the day-to-day routine of office administration. She co-ordinated all the departments, allowing me time to think and plan and look at the bigger picture.

Claudia Newton, filling the last vacancy for secretarial support, did me proud. She came on board at a most difficult time in the company's life when the merger with Soft Sheen had started to go wrong. She brought to the table her unique professional skills of office management that were to restore the company's image which was severely dented after Soft Sheen's involvement in the business. She became a tower of strength and supported me way beyond the call of duty.

I owe these ladies an immeasurable debt of gratitude and choose this page to acknowledge that they have been the backbone of my administration.

Influencing change was, in the broadest sense, perhaps by far the most significant of all the benefits that have accrued to the community as a whole. The business became a model for mentoring some of our young people. The 'can-win' attitude represented a mild revolution in the struggle for empowerment and became an important lesson to be taken seriously.

In the second place, it provided a seedbed for the development of a range of skills training and managerial experience that were to benefit the individuals working within the company and the community and the economy as a whole.

A further important economic dimension to this community self-start effort brought into play the multiplier effect with several past members of staff who were to become business owners and managers in their own right, and become involved in the process of wealth creation further extending the enterprise culture into the next generation.

Employment policy for the company had as its golden rule: 'selection of the best candidate for the job' with positively no discrimination along colour lines. This policy landed me into confrontation with several of my black customers who wanted to know why I was employing white people when there were so many black people out of work.

This was a pointedly difficult question but a good one and I had no hesitation in explaining the merits of the policy. We were an 'equal-opportunity' employer and the white employees that were being complained about were, as a matter fact, the best people for the job, with proven skills and experience for the positions they held. They filled a critical need within the organisation, and were in fact much more important to the company than appeared on the surface.

Quite apart from being the best qualified persons for the positions, their employment also represented part of my strategic aim to change attitudes by setting an example for corporate Britain. Challenging discrimination in the workplace was a major concern for us all, and here I had on my side the moral high ground that I had used and continue to use in challenging racism in employment and in the society.

This explanation was acceptable by most questioners who agreed with me after pointing out some of the opportunities opened up both in the private and public sector for influencing change which, at the end of the day, had helped to make for important inroads in certain positions in society generally.

A common problem faced by many young and highly qualified black people leaving school or university to enter the world of work for the first time was the lack of experience. The point to note was, that virtually all application forms asked for experience as a requirement before they could be considered.

This was an issue that I challenged whenever the opportunity presented itself. How could anyone have experience coming out of school? It was a grossly unfair system and a vicious circle. It became another area of company policy to offer work experience where possible to school leavers and graduates as they set out to find work. It was an approach that worked, one that made a difference for many new entrants into the world of work.

These company initiatives became a model of excellence for others to follow. Understanding how this worked in the interest of the community will become clearer as my involvement in the wider private and public sector unfold.

The black hair-care industry expanded rapidly from its small beginnings to the point where it became a magnet for new entrants into the industry. My office had by then become a sort of consultancy clearing house.

As the leading player in the industry at the time, it was also necessary for me to keep an eye on the competitors who focussed on our every move. The company was vigilant and understood only too well that we could not stand still. This would have been a certain recipe for disaster and so it continued to be innovative and diversified within the territory in which we operated.

Hindsight is a great teacher and learning from one's failure to make the right move at the right time can be costly. But being creative was a major strength and putting our customers first was of primary importance. I quote from the Commandments of Good Business Practice, my standard text for customer care:

> A customer is the most important person in any business; a customer is not dependent on us, we are dependent on him; a customer is not an interruption of our work, he/she is the purpose of it. A customer does us a favour when he/she calls; we do not do him a favour serving him. A customer is a part of our business, not an outsider. A customer is not someone to argue with or match wits with; a customer is someone who brings us his wants, which it is our job to fill. A customer is the life-blood of every business--the person who pays OUR WAGES.'

I strongly believe in these words of wisdom and have lived by them. It was advice I invited my staff to follow, and a recommendation that I made to the many emerging small businesses within the black community.

The Corporate Animal

Taming this inanimate beast took some doing. It was a question of the old adage holding true: Necessity is the mother of invention. If the need to succeed is strong enough, the learning curve for the required skills to get things done quickly falls into place. This has been my experience. Sourcing was a key plank in the business plan that took me to several parts of the USA where the industry was already well advanced. Implementing this part of my plan meant making contact on a one-to-one basis with my opposite numbers in the US where the products were manufactured. This was a top priority.

Meeting with the captains of the industry was a truly enlightening experience and, more importantly, gaining their support for my mission. My needs at our initial meetings were for stock and some credit facility. To my astonishment the credit was forthcoming without any resistance on their part. Clearly, I succeeded in selling them the huge opportunities that the UK market offered, which at that time was virgin territory. I drove home my argument that stocking their product lines represented an investment in the future of their businesses in my market.

I also staked my reputation on the line, pointing out that failing in our agreement would be detrimental to building my company's credit-worthiness, something which, at all times, I aimed to protect. This went down well with them and I made sure to honour the undertakings given. Indeed, I stood for nothing less, and along the way I was to benefit enormously from living up to my assurances.

This approach was strategic in every sense of the word, for during the period of the company's fastest growth, and the difficulties it experienced with UK banks, it was supplier credit that kept the momentum going. Confidence was built in most cases where agency agreements were established, albeit on a purely informal basis. This, as it happened, was a major error due to my inexperience and to being too trusting. I will deal with the consequences of this later.

The critical path that led to a small store in North London becoming nationally and internationally known for the widest selection of ethnic hair-care products to satisfy the needs of the black community had down roots at 43 West Green Road.

Providing the same service to other areas of the country was the natural thing to do. This move led to the opening of seven additional stores in different locations. The stores eventually became separate business units and were the forerunners in the company's growth.

Phase two of moving the company ahead was to get into shipping volume across the country. This was a progressive step that brought about the development of the distribution and exporting sides of the company. The experiment worked brilliantly and soon required a system to facilitate this leap forward. Adequate warehousing, transport and personnel were also required to deal with what became a major turning point in the company's advancement.

The logistics of supplying the major towns outside of London called for appointing sub–distributors in all the major cities of the midlands and the north to fill gaps in the distribution chain.

Expansion of the industry meant that during the late seventies and early eighties, every growth projection recorded a double-digit increase in turnover and tested the skills of management to its limits. Space became a constraint in satisfactorily managing the company's inventory. Two freeholds and one leasehold property were acquired.

These acquisitions offered a brief respite, but it was not long before the wholesale and export division had outgrown all three sites. Unfortunately, my judgement in accurately forecasting the space needs was widely underestimated and, for the third time, the business was bursting at the seams and we had to be on the lookout for adequate space from which to operate.

George Ellis & Co, the local estate agent who found our earlier properties, was again approached to find a much larger place. They came to the rescue with a 16,500 sq. ft. freehold property at 19 Bernard Road on the Rangemoor Industrial Estate, Tottenham, three times the area of what we had before. This acquisition met our needs nicely, allowing the company, for the first time, to work in comfort with state-of-the-art equipment to manage its operations.

The building provided good administrative offices for its directors and staff, with ample storage space and an excellent loading and unloading facility that made a difference by improving productivity. In addition, there was a proper showroom, a 'cash and carry' for the convenience of traders wishing to collect their purchases. A classroom and seminar room for promotions by manufacturers rounded off what became a prime business location for serving the industry.

The company's most strategic move, however, was its break-through into manufacturing. While all its other activities were building bricks of prosperity, manufacturing gave it an independence that had far-reaching ramifications that were to set the company even further ahead in the industry.

Its success had spawned other players to enter the industry, vigorously swimming after the leader. This meant that staying ahead was an ever-present challenge to be faced. As the market matured and competition increased, it was important to become less dependent on suppliers who for fear of losing market share, began to renege on their verbal agreements with the company.

Predictably, as I was to discover, handshake agreements were useless, for my assumed loyalty went out the window as new business outlets in direct competition with the company were opened.

It was, in a way, like being at war for despite the fact that Dyke & Dryden had carried the cost of opening up the market at colossal expense from which they all benefited, it made no difference whatever to their ruthlessness. It was a rude awakening and a tough lesson to learn, that conducting business on nothing more than a handshake is bad business practice. Hindsight is a great teacher but, unfortunately, always too late in showing its face.

The fierce onslaught from my previously good friends was in a way understandable, for the pupil had now become a competitor in production, an area that was once their exclusive territory. This upstart had to be challenged. Sabotage of our operations was not unknown, including several attempts to buy us out before we were ready to quit.

A critical review of the company's position was well under way in the attempt to protect our place in the industry. Manufacturing our own products was the answer.

Joan, my first secretary, was articulate, ambitious and had the habit of bouncing her ideas off me. One day, exactly what I feared happened, she gave me notice of her intention to leave for a new career. She wanted to become a hairdresser, she explained. My immediate response was to offer her encouragement. I explained just how much I would miss her, but asked her to promise me one thing-- that after her training she would come back and see me. She did.

'What are your plans now?' I enquired. 'I would like to open a salon but have no capital' she responded. 'As long as you are willing to have me as a partner in your business', I replied, 'you can start looking for premises.' She revealed later that she could not believe what she was hearing. Satisfied from our earlier work together that her motivation dictated that anything she put her mind to would succeed, my backing her was a foregone conclusion.

No time was lost in finding suitable premises, which I approved in tandem with founding Supreme Hairdressers Ltd at Turnpike Lane, London N8 with Joan as Company Secretary and Technical Director, and myself as Managing Director. The salon prospered followed in quick succession by Supreme School of Hair Design. Joan became my prodigy and we made a great team as business partners.

Joan was innovative and hard-working and within a year both the salon and school had impacted on the industry in such a way that their reputations quickly became nationally and internationally known, attracting patrons from everywhere, especially from many parts of Africa.

The school in particular was strategic in every sense of the word by turning out students who were soon to become the new generation of hairdressers, not only for Britain, but for other parts of the world from which many of its students came.

The salon and school were a strategic tactical move that was to support the Dyke & Dryden's product development programme. Joan's technical know-how in products application and in the salon, was invaluable in working alongside the contract packing laboratories we used for development work in the testing of our products.

It was a remarkable breakthrough in the building of linkages across each of our business segments. Free hairdos made for a ready supply of clients who volunteered to have their hair worked on using Super Curl. At the same time students were taught how to use the company's products. These events were unique in the marketing mix in building the customer base and loyalty.

The Super Curl brand could not have come on stream at a more opportune time. It was an instant winner. Hair fashions were in the throws of a revolution, sporting what became known as the curly look, the wet look and the wavy look. The product was used for men's hairstyles and was referred to in some circles as the 'executive look'.

The process was simple enough. The use of thioglycolic acid, the active ingredient in the gel perm, breaks down the sulphur dioxide bonds of the hair, which enables change in its natural configuration, from small, tight curls to the desired size and shape or whatever might be the craze at the time.

Chemical processing, by its very nature, causes substantial moisture loss and, therefore, has to be replaced by daily doses of moisturising treatments to stop the hair from breaking. The need for intensive use of the after-care products made for large volume sales in 'curl products' and carried excellent margins. It was therefore the ambition of every manufacturer to be in on providing curl after-care treatments.

Super Curl became a leading brand and a firm favourite in several world markets, in particular Nigeria, the largest of them all generating volume sales that accounted for 30 per cent of the company's turnover. The phenomenal success of Super Curl gave rise to a second brand using the same formula save for perfume and colour differences under the brand name of Curl Control.

This happened to be a spectacular tactical piece of manoeuvring, for, as it turned out, while both brands were competing against each other, they carved out for the company the largest share of the trade in the curl market.

In Holland, Curl Control ruled the waves so completely that pirating became a common occurrence and steps had to be taken to track down the pirates. To have our products copied because of how well they were doing was flattering, but when it hurts your pocket it becomes a different ball game altogether.

Suspicion was centred on a member of staff at the factory where the products were contract packed, and our investigators after being armed with a search warrant for the home of the suspect, found the mould used by the perpetrator hidden under his bed!

Examination of the mould showed that they had done a perfect copy and until they were stopped at great expense, it was difficult to determine our losses through piracy. New methods of protecting the brands were developed, and to the best of my knowledge, the problem ceased. The product lines were expanded to cover all the essential items used daily and became household names.

Not all attempts at manufacturing were successful though, as the following episode will clearly show. The ethnic market was small beer compared to the huge white marketplace on which I always had an eye and I came out with a product suitable for entering it. This was a cocoa butter cream and lotion under our Natural Beauty brand that stood a good chance of success in this market, given a level playing field. But it was not to be.

I contracted with a company in Aldershot to produce the items that were unique to the segment of the market we were targeting. Jane Hammond, our consultant at Trident Public Relations Ltd, delivered a great line in our press release on the new product. It read: 'A beauty secret known to generations of Caribbean women is now available in the UK to pamper the delicate skins of English women, thanks to Dyke & Dryden.'

Jane's message was bang on cue, producing excellent feedback from our target market, the white population. Among the regular users were our bank manager's wife and her daughters who loved the creams and were regularly supplied. Our generous sampling campaigns did well in creating demand. I knew too, from inside information, that we were on to a winner for the women at the factory where the products were produced, (who were all white) loved our products and switched to our creams and lotions in preference to those they had used before.

There were however two major hurdles. The first was to find a distributor in the mainstream with national distribution outlets willing to carry the line, and secondly, the project needed additional funding. The return on investment on the new lines carried good margins, and the distributors approached expressed a willingness to carry them once they could be assured of regular supplies.

We were, it seemed, on the verge of a new dawn of getting into the big white market, what seemed a win-win situation, with a unique product for which there was unmistakeable demand, and with distribution in place. Sadly, our bank manager although being involved in every detail of the project up to the point of our successful market testing by his own sources, failed to provide the funding.

This was a deadly blow. Some months after his refusal to fund the project, an identical product appeared in a number of high street stores in the country under a different brand name carrying the identical copy that I had written. Was it sabotage? I could not confirm it, but everything pointed in that direction. It was a tough lesson. The breakthrough for which I had worked really hard was within my grasp, if only our bank's support had been forthcoming. 'You have enough to get on with,' my bank manager had declared.

Marketing the company's brands was an absolute necessity if we were to continue to grow and improve our market share. A variety of focussed marketing campaigns were put together both for the home and overseas markets.

On the home front, some market campaigns were great party occasions, full of fun with an array of young, beautiful girls eager to be selected as models or to be included in hair demonstrations. Above and below the line, marketing was employed in varying degrees in all our campaigns. Standard formats included posters placed in selected sites in the London underground, on billboards with product shots, in specialist magazines and in newspapers.

We piloted placing product shots on our output of yearly calendars and made a habit of giving them to as many of our customers as we could as a thank-you with Christmas gifts, and this was well received. Customers showed their appreciation and looked forward to collecting their calendars each year.

This method of marketing proved a particularly effective way of bringing our products to the attention of the public throughout the calendar's useful life over the whole year. This was especially so in parts of Africa. It was no surprise to see the competition following our lead.

Product launches had an air of what came to be known as 'The Show'. Specialist choreographers brought special skills to bear on the event and pulled things together in a way that created lots of excitement for a public that adored the razzle-dazzle of these events. The creativity of the many artists and art forms on show, were later to become the fashions of the day!

This tried and trusted format, after being well rehearsed in the UK at Afro Hair & Beauty, was taken overseas where 'The Show' went down as a treat in the huge markets of Nigeria, Uganda, Kenya and Ghana. It was as I predicted—manufacturing would turn out to be the company's most formidable asset over time.

The Nigerian market, by virtue of its size, bought huge volumes of all our products. I got to know many of the big trading names in Lagos and elsewhere, places where I made some lasting friendships. If Napoleon's reference to 'a nation of shopkeepers' was applied to Nigeria, it would be most appropriate. Try any day of the week you care to brave through Bologun Market and you cannot help but come to that conclusion.

Nigerian women control trading in Bologun Market, Lagos and I daresay this control extends to all the other markets as well. The country is rich in cultural diversity and to understand and absorb it, you almost need the mind of a scientist.

My findings in West and East Africa were much the same, but for their individual cultural differences. Ghana for example, though a much smaller country, compared with Nigeria spends more per head on beauty treatments than her neighbour.

Ghananian women are the trendsetters in hair fashion and to attend their hair-care needs with a passion akin to religious fervour. Tema Hairdressers' Association and Hairway Beauty Clinic jointly hosted a reception for my technical team and myself in June 1986, with a presentation titled 'Natural Beauty Day'. This was a workshop in Accra to promote our Natural Beauty Products. The energy in the crowded workshop was electrifying as eager students sought to improve their skills and knowledge of the profession.

Mrs Eesi Sutherland, Under Secretary for Culture and Tourism, in her opening remarks set the tone for the day. She reminded the hairdressers that they were the trendsetters for whatever was the fashion of the day and that she wanted to see workshops conducted all over the country. The workshop was a great success on two fronts--sharing educational know-how, and the marketing of our brands in the process.

A big thank-you went to Bertha Bohemaa for organising the event, while a donation of 100,000 cedars was presented to the Under Secretary for Labour and Social Welfare, Mr T. K. Owusu, to aid the treatment of women in psychiatric hospitals.

It was a very humbling experience in all the countries I visited to find a common acceptance of our brands across the entire continent. Credit for this phenomenal success is due to Afro Hair & Beauty, the exhibition I founded in 1982. Afro Hair & Beauty is regarded as the 'shop window to the world'. Like a magnet, it draws unto itself traders from across the Atlantic and throughout the diaspora. Traders from Africa with their old colonial trading links still intact, found shopping in the UK easy and the company's establishments were compulsory stops!

American corporations saw the exhibition as their key marketplace and invaded the event in great numbers, bringing with them a huge range of products, new technology and the promotional tools that went with the merchandise they offered. They were big spenders and sought to dominate the event by using their spending power to create displays that were attractive. They eventually walked away with the awards for the most creative stand which became a coveted prize at the exhibition.

The exhibition's launch at the prestigious five-star Governor House Hotel in Park Lane in 1982 was a trail-blazing affair, opened by Lady Dorothy Pitt, the darling of the black community and an ardent supporter of black enterprise. In her opening remarks, she reminded her audience, that 'black is beautiful and we must never be tired of saying so and showing how true it is.'

Justifiably, pride and self-esteem characterised her remarks. The exhibition is now in its 25th year, has become an important date in the black community's business/social calendar, and remains a cornerstone and incubator for building black enterprise in Britain.

During the early years of the exhibition, hair and skin products together with fashion and associated items were the beginning of what has now grown into a broad-based showplace which includes a wide variety of products and services demanded by the public at large.

Corporate Britain has now recognised the importance of the exhibition and has accordingly slotted it a place in the country's tourist manual for visitors to Britain. Public companies, training bodies, banks and even the Inland Revenue use the event to convey their messages to different sections of the public.

In purely economic terms, the industry promotes employment for many thousands of people. There are over 1,000 hairdressing salons employing on average two to three persons which translates to approximately over 3,000 jobs. In retailing, with more than 2,000 stores selling ethnic beauty products with staff levels at between three and four persons per store, accounting on average for a further 6,000 jobs.

If we were to add the jobs to those in sales, hairdressing schools, manufacturing, warehousing, distribution and exporting, management, accountancy, marketing and promotion, it becomes clear to see the multiplier effect on employment, and the profound impact of the industry on the lives of many families.

At this juncture it is worth recalling some of the highlights of the events that mark their place in history and I quote the *West Indian World* of Wednesday May 1, 1985. 'Europe's largest exhibition for black hair care and cosmetics industry comes to Wembley'. The writer goes on, 'seven weeks to go—and Afro Hair & Beauty '85 at Wembley on June 1 and 2, after all those crowds the first two years in London hotel ballrooms, you'll have much more room to move—as well as lots more to see.'

Another publication, the *Asian Times* reported, 'Afro Hair & Beauty was set to break records this year with forty companies who have already reserved space, and as many more have also expressed an interest in taking part, which suggests a bumper year for the Exhibition.' The forecasts were correct in one respect only.

The numbers of companies exhibiting had tripled, but alas, the heavens opened and the show was a wash out. The attendance did not live up to what was expected and many pockets were left with gaping holes in them. There was no insurance cover to take account of this act of God and Afro Hair & Beauty itself ended up with a whopping loss that year of £43,000.00. It was one of those setbacks that goes with the business and had to be taken on board courageously.

In planning forward for Afro Hair & Beauty '86, it was felt that the distance for many travellers was too far out from the centre of town, and that certainly did not help the '85 show. A new purpose-built venue, the Business Design Centre located in Islington, North London, was found which was much nearer the centre and, for the time being, fitted the bill nicely.

Unfortunately, its crowd-holding capacity fell far short of accommodating the huge crowds the show attracted. It was soul-destroying to see long lines of patrons lining up unable to be admitted and having to be turned away. The popularity of the event was such that a new venue had to be found to cope with the sheer numbers that attended the show.

After two years of overcrowding at the Business Design Centre, a new home was eventually found at Alexander Palace in Wood Green, which met in full the overwhelming demand for additional space. This is a unique and exquisite facility, full of history and set in 196 acres of parkland, which offers a multiplicity of interesting options for the great and important event which, from its humble beginnings, it has become.

The event has over the years become institutionalised, falling on specific calendar days. The bank holiday weekend at the end of May is a great weekend out for entire families. Opportunities galore exist to explore what is new and interesting at the many fashion and hair shows, educational seminars, or simply on the lookout bargains or just to hang out with friends. Whatever the interest, the event remains a centrepiece for the community.

Staff Who Were Pillars of Strength

Pat Parkinson
*Computer Sales
Invoicing Clerk*

Pearl Goodridge who managed my office and doubled as Personnel Manager. She was my 'eyes and ears' during the phenomenal growth of the business.

Kingsley Peters
Chief Accountant

Claudia Newton – a tower of secretarial strength in the difficult times after I bought the company back from Soft Sheen.

Paulette Grier – a pillar of support during visits while I worked abroad in Nigeria.

Memorable Occassions

The Women in Business seminar presentation of two 50.00 prizes by NLBDA's chairman to two runners-up of the 'Best Enterprising Presentation'

Guest of Prime Minister Margaret Thatcher with wife Roslyn Wade at Number 10, Downing Street – February 1984

(left front row) In attendance looking on is Mr Mike Nixon, Chief Executive of the North London Training and Enterprise Council.

Making a point at a black business conference – seated left Mr. Colin Carter Secretary of the (UK) Caribbean Chamber of Commerce and member of Parliament Mr. John McGregor Small Firms Minister.

(L to R) George Napper (Atlanta Police Chief), J.C. Douglas (M & M Products) and Tony Wade (Dyke & Dryden)

A.E.S. Wade, MBE, Chairman, presents the NLBDA Community Award to Sir Peter Imbert.

Fun Times in
Australia and Egypt

Cruising on the Nile in Egypt

Day out at the Brisbane Zoo

Sightseeing with Vasantha and her sister Giri Cuttle in Brisbane Australia

Camel-riding in Egypt

On the Brisbane River with my father-in-law S. M. Warria and Vasantha

Memorable walks with Vasantha along Gold Coast in Australia

More Memorable Occassions

In conversation with President Daniel Arap Moi at a Dyke & Dryden business promotion in Kenya.

Tony Wade with daughter Deborah

Priscilla Duberry – who cared for my children and managed my home after the passing of my late wife, Daphne

Receiving the award of a Fellow of the Elegant Twins School of Hairdressing from Mrs Elizabeth Osinsanya at a double celebration of her Golden Jubilee 1953–2003. (50 years in business and marriage)

Lord Bill Morris & publisher Arif Ali at book launch of 'How They Made A Million'.

Mrs. Jean Sadler presenting a cheque to representatives from the Jamaica Cancer Society – proceeds of the "Daphne Wade Cancer Fund".

Some Great Social Events

Guest on the occasion of the Presentation Launch of the Royal Yachts stamp series in honour of the Royal Wedding of H.R.H The Prince of Wales to Lady Diana Spencer - London Hilton Hotel 1981

At the launch of 'Black Enterprise in Britain' Dame Jocelyn Barrow and Stephen O'Brien.

Welcoming Baroness Denton of Wakefield at a NLBDA Conference in Hackney. Looking on is Emmanuel Cotter, Chief Executive Officer of NLBDA.

The Princess Royal at opening of the North London Business Development Agency – Home secretary David Waddington & Lord Boardman, Chairman of NATWEST.

Family Moments

Sister Mavis and brother James Wade.

A family get together at home in Vista Del Mar.

Aqasa, Sheveta and bridesmaids at the wedding

A memorable moment with my new daughter

A photo opportunity at the London Guild Hall 2005 on the event of my 'Lifetime Achievement in Business Award' with my wife Vasantha, flanked by Olga Try left, Margaret Alexander and Philip Try right.

93

Marketing My Company's Brands in Ghana

Ghanaian models promoting Super Curl in Accra.

Hairdressers and students at a seminar in Accra.

Wonderful Social Events

My father-in-law's former staff at "Chemara Research Station" Seremban, Malaysia entertain us at a local restaurant. (1997)

His Excellency Emmanuel Cotter MBE, his wife Stephanie and Sir Peter and Lady Imbert joined me in celebrating Mr. Cotter's distinguished services to the London Business Development Agency.

A cricket Bat......

... with a £500,000 pounds tag on it.

A Cricket Bat

This particular bat is an object with a £500,000 tag on it. It takes pride of place in my home. It seems unreal and unbelievable that a piece of willow, crafted, treated, and polished has for centuries remained an object of attachment for many and provides immeasurable pleasure and fascination for millions.

Gracing the top end of the bevelled face of this special piece of willow is in bold print a name known the world over by cricketing enthusiasts — Duncan Fearnley, Worcester, England. It sports a logo depicting wickets complete with bales jumping out at you. Neatly inscribed below are the words 'hand-made perfection' with the added claim of 'Supreme' in bold print.

This prized piece of willow differs from all others I have personally seen. Inscribed on the blade are the signatures of sporting heroes. Heroes, now legendary. They featured in the series England versus the West Indies 1984 at a time when West Indians dominated world cricket.

Dominate is the only appropriate verb when one looks back at the decisive beating England got in the series. The history of the beating is catalogued as follows: First test at Edgebaston, Windies won by an innings and 180 runs; at Lords, won by 9 wickets; at Headingley, won by 8 wickets; at Old Trafford, won by an innings and 64 runs; and at the Oval a final win by 172 runs! A blackwash if ever there was one!

It might be as well to name the members of the teams on the trophy. The sporting English team included captain David Gower, Allan Lamb, Nick Cook, G. Fowler, B.C. Broad, A.J. Lamb, M.W. Gatting, I.T. Botham, P.R. Downton, D.R. Pringle and R.G. Willis.

The victorious Windies included captain Clive Lloyd, Jeffry Dujon, Michael Holding, C.G. Greenidge, D.L. Haynes, H.A. Gomes, M.D. Marshall, E.A. Baptise, R.A. Harper, J. Garner, and V.A. Richards.

An accident during my schoolboy cricketing days brought an abrupt end to the boyhood ambition of one day being selected to play for the West Indies. Instead, I have been forced to live in the glory of others, resigned to spectator status only. Endearing shots I could only dream about crossed my mind constantly – cracking fours and sixes to the boundary, pulling onto leg, cutting into the slips, or defensively showing a determined bowler the blade.

This prized piece of willow somehow satisfies that longing in a strange sort of way. It was to begin with, a 'wager' that was to convert false perception into normal business ethics and redeem two souls from unexplained bigotry and subsequently to purge themselves of thoughts once harboured.

A company based in Bradford (which shall be nameless) was famous for producing hair products. After some persuasion the company reluctantly agreed to take a chance to contract pack for my company. This confession by the chairman of the company was made only after the spectacular success of a project they had reluctantly agreed to do.

Both father and son like most Yorkshire men were ardent cricket lovers and well connected with the hierarchy who managed the sport. As such, they had access to all the frills that the cricket citadel of Lords could offer.

It was no accident that the son had as one of his prized possessions a much sought after autographed 1984 bat that occupied pride of place among the trophies in his home. As our business grew, so too did our friendship. One day at his home, he showed off his treasured piece of willow to me with a challenge.

'Your purchases,' he said beaming with undisguised delight, 'from my company in 1985 amounted to £250,000 for that year. If in any one year you were to spend £500,000 with me,' he challenged, 'that trophy could be yours.' He was serious.

Not one for ducking a challenge, I took him on and the following year 1986, I spent with him £800,000, almost doubling the figure of his wager. With the figures verified, I promptly made my way to his home and collected his precious bat, which today occupies no less a pride of place in my home than it had from whence it came! My good friend as he eventually became cheerfully handed over his precious willow to me, but I suspect he wished he had never made the wager!

In the meantime, his father admitted how they almost lost the opportunity of a lifetime, 'simply by being bigots'. Our business grew to a point where they became our largest supplier and we in turn their biggest customer. The friendship and goodwill that came out of taking a chance to say the least was quite remarkable, and they subsequently thanked me for making them millionaires.

The major lesson from this episode in my journey was that it had made a difference – had changed the mindset and perception held about other people's abilities and become an outcome for good.

A Celebration

The year 1985 was a landmark in the company's history and called for a celebration. September marked our twentieth year in business and was an occasion to reflect and give thanks.

We had to celebrate 20 years of good fortune and of being lucky enough to have had the support of a loyal team of senior managers. They were the people who made our progress possible. These people have never been absent from my thoughts and I will always have great respect for them. I think of three persons in particular, Pearl Goodridge, Rudi Page and Kingsley Peter.

Pearl managed my office in a most competent manner; she seemed to read my mind, keeping time wasters at bay. She was a trusted confidant and allowed me the freedom to look at the big picture and not be bogged down with detail.

In the marketplace Rudi, as Sales and Marketing Manager, lived up to the huge weight of responsibility his office carried and put in motion the important task of masterminding our brand-awareness strategy. This was a key imperative to his success. Kingsley, my Finance Director, was in a class all by himself as he tightly championed control of the company's finances. The zeal and commitment of these gentlemen went beyond the call of duty as I left them entirely free to design and organise the celebrations.

On Sunday, September 15, the celebrations kicked off with a short thanksgiving service at the Community Church of God in Tottenham, London N15, the borough in which the company had been founded. The Reverend Martin Goodridge MA and Father Lamont Philips conducted the service to a packed congregation, which included members of staff and supporters from across London.

Party celebrations began on Saturday, September 21, with a disco at the company's head office for staff andmembers of their families and friends. This was the warm-up for the formal event that was to follow at the famous Chanticleer banqueting rooms on Paxton Road, Tottenhan N17.

Full community participation in the event was the number one consideration, and the organising committee recognised the important role the community had played in the coming of age of the company.

Representatives of all segments of the industry from across the Atlantic were in attendance and presented their tributes and awards. So too were civic and public figures. For the company, it was the most appropriate opportunity to say a public 'thank you' to the dedicated staff who had made the difference. The attached letter summarises the feelings of all those who attended the ceremony.

HARINGEY COMMUNITY RELATIONS COUNCIL

14A Turnpike Lane
Wood Green
London N8 0PT
01—889 6871/2

your ref:

our ref:

RECEIVED 2 3 SEP 1985

17th September 1985

Messers Dyke, Dryden & Wade,
Directors,
Dyke and Dryden Ltd.,
93 West Green Road,
London N15.

Dear Sirs,

Re: Twentieth Year in Business

Haringey Community Relations Council wish to congratulate you and your
staff, as well as to wish you future success on attaining 20 years in
business.

This is an achievement which must have meant foresight, dedication
and hard work.

One cannot but admire and compliment you as directors of your company for as
equally making valuable contributions, to the well being and welfare of our
local communities while at the same time gaining National and International
recognition.

We are indeed proud and delighted that your success and achievement has
not removed you from associating yourselves, and identifying with the every
day needs and problems of ordinary people.

Your achievements must of necessity create a high standard of self awareness
for the Black Community and particularly so "Black Youngsters".

Accept our silent toast to the good health and happiness of yourselves and
staff, as well as the continued success of the company, and all who share
and identify in it now and in future years.

God bless you all.

On behalf of Haringey Community Relations Council.

Yours sincerely,

Chris Kavallares
Chairman

102

The Succession

One of the major failings of the majority of black-owned businesses is in not successfully making the transition from a first-generation business to the second. This is a noticeable feature in the US as well.

Of my own generation, examples are to be found among several of the large successful corporations with whom I have done business, among them Soft Sheen Products, M & M Products, Proline Products and Johnson Products. The consequences of this adverse regressive state of affairs are easily calculated. Capital accumulation, the basis of economic empowerment achieved usually at a high human cost, is lost to the community.

An attempt to avoid this pitfall remains for me one of the saddest episodes of my business life. Strategies for the succession were considered. A clearly detailed programme was to bring on board two young men who were of an age to learn the business and to take it forward into the future. These two young men were mature enough to understand the importance of their assignment. It was for them in truth an opportunity on a platter. After in-depth interviews and their firm expression of willingness to become part of the organisation they were placed in key departments for training.

One was being trained to shadow me. He had a persuasive personality, a valuable asset for anyone working in an industry whose success depends on an element of vanity. The quality of the products and services offered must however also meet the reasonable expectations of customers and, in this connection, satisfaction was of paramount importance as a matter of company policy.

I did my level best to groom my charge for the post of Chief Executive and was comfortable in the belief that I had achieved a measure of success that when the time came, he would relieve me of my daily responsibilities. Having mastered the daily routine well, he was given greater responsibility.

Over time, however, his performance started to slip. It was difficult to understand how someone who had showed such promise could suddenly begin to lose a grip on what was, after all, in his best interest. He suddenly seemed to have lost his way.

Ronald Hagman of Hagman Laboratories, one of my contract packers, telephoned that his company urgently wanted a meeting with me about my shadow and I naturally responded quickly as requested. I had given Ronald authority to supply my understudy with any orders that he presented.

At our meeting I was horror-struck. Ronald presented me with a range of products outside the brands produced for us. He had only become aware of what was going on when he was advised that the invoices for the new products were to be given to my understudy in person, not sent to the office in the normal way.

Moreover, my trusted understudy had arranged for the goods to be collected by our trucks and sold to our customers on the driver's rounds. There could be only one response – it was a case of gross misconduct that called for immediate dismissal.

But much worse was to follow. Copies of all our business secrets had ended up in the hands of a customer who eventually became our fiercest competitor, and the next thing I knew was that my understudy would become my competitor's right-hand man. So much for loyalty!

My other trainee understudied the warehouse manager. This being the area that husbands the company's wealth, one needed eyes in the back of the head. He turned out to be a square peg in a round hole and had to be relieved of his position and transferred to sales in an effort to try and make something of him.

Other candidates for the succession did not start. They were intent on dictating their own terms of engagement, something which could not be entertained. These episodes between them had put an end to the possibility of a succession. This story is told in the hope that it may alert a future generation to the dangers inherent in the failure to protect one's inheritance.

The (UK) Caribbean Chamber of Commerce

Over the years, I have been involved in various organisations that have actively worked towards achieving a more equitable and harmonious society. One such organisation was the UK Caribbean Chamber of Commerce.

The Chamber became one of the most influential black organisations in Britain. It was in the forefront of the effort for black business advancement with a membership representative of businesses and the professions. It led the campaign to increase black business involvement in the society.

Colin Carter, Managing Director of Jet Load Trading, and I became members at the same time and did our best to build an organisation of which our community could be justly proud.

Upon joining the organisation we were both voted into office, Colin as Chamber Secretary and I as Deputy Chair under the distinguished leadership of Pal Ganguli who managed the Red Stripe organisation in the UK at the time. When Pal was recalled for business in India and had to resign, I succeeded him.

Shortly after being installed into office Colin and I discovered that the Chamber's organisational structure left much to be desired in that it operated out of Pal's office with no staff of its own. These were issues we both agreed had to be addressed with the utmost urgency. To be effective, the organisation needed a home and staff of its own and we duly placed these matters on the table for discussion with the management committee.

The committee accepted our recommendation that the time had come for the Chamber to assert its independence and operate from premises of its own. These steps had an immediate effect on the organisation's standing for they brought ease of access, visibility and suitable office accommodation with meeting rooms. It represented a giant leap forward.

Carter as General Secretary was energetic, perceptive and committed to this work. He was always on top of the officers' performance and the discharge of their duties and ensured that policy decisions taken by the Board were carried out in a professional and timely manner. As a past soldier, he was strong on discipline and often succeeded in getting the best out of the staff. He was a first-rate team player who could always be relied upon to make what seemed impossible, possible.

Between us, we had charted a path that earned great respect for the Chamber's aspirations and drive for change. One initiative in particular stands out, which may be worth mentioning for the benefit of students dealing with research on racial disadvantage. The Chamber's submission was titled 'Evidence and recommendation to the House of Commons, Home Affairs Parliamentary Sub-Committee on Race Relations December 1980'. This document may be found in the Home Office library and I have naturally kept a personal copy.

In the course of the Chamber's affairs, I made many speeches in Britain. One which I recall with a little pride was delivered at the Café Royal in London in the presence of the Right Honourable John Wheeler MP, Home Office Minister with responsibility for matters dealing with migrants. There was also a large number of other distinguished guests at the function, the occasion of the fifth anniversary of the Chamber. The following is an extract of my speech that evening:

> 'Tonight, ladies and gentlemen, represents another landmark in the Chamber's history. History is a story of past changes, parts of which are more important than others – not because they were shorter or longer, but because the changes taking place at a particular time more profoundly affect the lives of people since then. I believe that the (UK) Caribbean Chamber of Commerce is on the threshold of such a change.

> The Garveyist spirit of self-help, enterprise and risk-taking is characteristic of West Indians and of our general attitude to work. It was this spirit, in the first place, which brought us to Britain. We genuinely believed that if we worked hard and competed, economic success would be assured--without realising however, that these alone were not sufficient to create viable economies in

our communities. Rather, owning a stake in the British economy, with access and a level playing field are key imperatives.

In the face of obstacles, we must therefore prepare to gird our loins, and use every opportunity to utilise our skills and distinctive competencies to create and build our own businesses, our own markets and ultimately create our own wealth. The stark reality is that we live in a commercial and industrial society and all our actions must be informed by this fact. I believe that our whole socio-political status as a community will, at the end of the day, depend on our ability to maintain and sustain our basic interests.

We cannot hope to improve our place in society by being left sitting on the fringe of society, oblivious to what is happening around us. We must stake our claim and make our presence felt. The importance of a sound community economic base cannot be overstated. It is the whole purpose of what our Chamber is all about. Some of us have taken on the role of pioneers in areas that present real challenges--in manufacturing, distribution and some service industries. Tonight my friends, I urge you to let us keep before us our objectives and our sense of purpose and to assert our rightful place in the society in which we toil. Only then, will our Chamber have fulfilled the historic mission that we have, together, undertaken.'

The UKCC fulfilled several key functions. It was essential for the business community to speak with one voice in dealing with institutions. It also filled the all-important role of being a resource centre for community businesses of all shapes and sizes. As far as the African and Caribbean communities were concerned, the importance of the Chamber may be summarised by a slight juggling of Voltaire's famous observation on the deity 'If there were no UKCC, it would have been supremely necessary to invent it.'

Community work at UKCC had become part of my life, working with like-minded friends to help to broaden our business base. This experience added a new dimension to my life: it provided a new understanding and a broader picture of local and national issues as they unfolded and affected us. I became even more people-centred and committed to work even harder as we struggled to face up to racism and financial ostracism.

As fate would have it, my old boss Louis Segal from my Smart Weston days was Chairman at the Islington Chamber of Commerce in the borough next door. News reached him that I was the new UKCC chair and, being the gentleman he was, he quickly invited me over for a chat and offered me the benefit of his years of experience which proved invaluable.

Serendipity, one of his gourmet restaurants in Camden Passage famous for its antiques shops, became a regular rendezvous for our meetings. This life's lesson has stayed with me, of how I became a beneficiary of his mentoring while employed by him at Smart Weston, and how he was later to remain my guru in yet another area of work.

In our meetings he advised on how to build our business networks, which could become useful financial building blocks for community progress. This was a message I reinforced and that the Chamber recognised, that without a structured financial capability to support community development, we would continue to wobble at the bottom of the economic ladder.

With this clear objective in mind, the Chamber served as a vehicle to articulate and spread the gospel that each member of the community must grasp the simple truth that the world does not owe us a living. It is we who must build wealth-creation strategies and work relentlessly to accomplish our objectives.

The following is yet another extract from my speech at our December annual general meeting (AGM) in 1982.

> 'In my address last year, members will recall that I said that we had succeeded in informing the financial institutions, both local and national of the difficulty our members encounter in raising business finance for start-up or expansion capital.
>
> The struggle for a better deal for our members remains a top priority. I believed then that we were on the

threshold of a break-through and today I am happy to present to you what I consider to be the cornerstone of the building of our business community.

Our own business development unit is now in place and functioning, and I want to publicly acknowledge and thank the Greater London Council (GLC) for making this possible. I would also like to pay tribute to our consultant, Martin Kazuka, who assisted us in many ways in preparing and presenting our application and by attending numerous meetings with GLC officials.

A similar application was made to the government for special funding. The nature of these discussions differed in scope from the GLC, in that here we were looking to government to make a commitment in like manner as the Senate Select Committee on Small Businesses did in the United States.

The Brixton Riots stirred the conscience of the nation and moved the leadership to act. Lord Scarman, the eminent judge who chaired the enquiry into the riots, was forthright in his report and his recommendations were accepted.'

Not only were the Chamber's views sought, but we were also given prime-time television exposure to present our case. Hugh Scully, the high profile BBC reporter, was my interviewer on *Nationwide* on April 6, 1982 in a live programme at 6:00 p.m. that evening. Hugh Scully's questioning sought to get to the root cause of black business under-achievement and appended below are some questions and answers from the interview.

Hugh Scully: Tony Wade, what is your chamber doing to address the problems your members face?

Tony Wade: We have, in the first place, set ourselves a programme of raising the level of business activity in our community to a membership of about 500 businesses over the next five years.

Hugh Scully: Will this make a difference?

Tony Wade: Yes it will, by sharing in the economic life of the country in a more meaningful way than it is at the moment.

Hugh Scully: If, for example, you were to travel to Southall, you would find almost all the businesses there are Asian-owned, why is this so?

Tony Wade: That's easy. Three situations are the cause. First of all, most of the business owners you will find there came from East Africa and brought with them huge cash resources amassed primarily in Uganda. Secondly, their resources, combined with their managerial experience, gave them a flying start. And thirdly, they also had the support of Asian and other banks. In the case of West Indians we had nothing and had to start from scratch and, as a consequence, have lagged behind.

Hugh Scully: You mention the banks, is there a problem there?

Tony Wade: Our banks have been less than supportive to our membership, and where there is nominal support the collateral requirements asked for are prohibitive. This paints a picture of the difficulties the community has had to endure.

In an attempt to try and address the reasons for our poor showing, my discussions with Ministers and officials were at the point of bearing fruit. I argued that from my discussions with several black businessmen in the US, the injection of public finance, together with set-aside contracts, had been the most important factor in giving black Americans a stake in the US economy, a proven formula which I am sure could have the same results here in the UK.

But at the point where I thought I had a government deal in the bag, the jockeys of disaster were at work. Like most fledgling bodies, the UKCC has had its share of opportunists and mercenaries. Some members were reluctant to work together to develop the chamber, while others undermined its work. These practices have no place in community development; they are destructive and must be firmly stamped out.

Among our major concerns were the effects of institutional racism in the financial services and the impact it had on our members. The Home Affairs Committee Report on Racial Disadvantage to which we gave evidence stated:

> 'It cannot be through equal access to employment opportunities alone that racial disadvantage is to be overcome, it is equally important that ethnic minority businessmen should be enabled to play a full part in the nation's economy as employers and self-employed.

> Not only does self-employment provide an alternative source of income, particularly important for those who are disadvantaged or discriminated against in the search for employment, but it also contributes to the regeneration of the urban areas in which the majority of ethnic minorities live. It is thus, in the interests of the whole community, that obstacles to full participation by members of any minority group in the creation and running of small businesses should be removed.'

That report highlighted and carried most of the Chamber's recommendations. However, it was Lord Scarman's Report on the Brixton riots that made the greatest impact. Among the things he said were the following:

> 'The encouragement of black people to secure a real stake in their own community, through business and the professions, is of great importance if future social stability is to be secured. I do urge the necessity for speedy action if we are to avoid the perpetuation in this country of an economically dispossessed black population.'

These views clearly expressed the ideals for which the Chamber stood, and for which we fought.

As I have already stated, the Chamber was on course for fulfilling its mission. Two weeks before the 1982 AGM I had a visit from a senior civil servant to discuss how the Chamber could be involved in taking forward Lord Scarman's recommendations. He explained to me that government had looked favourably on the achievements the Chamber had made and wanted to know if the Chamber would consider separating its business development arm to become part of the recommendations made by Lord Scarman.

I welcomed his suggestion and expressed my personal delight at this initiative. I informed him that I would communicate it to my committee, adding that we were one week away from our AGM and that it would be best dealt with after the election of new officers. The events that followed the election were to spell disaster for the Chamber and cause its demise.

Prior to the AGM, we had an intake of seventeen new members who had signalled their admiration for the Chamber's work and expressed their very keen interest in making a contribution. Contrary to our usual custom of vetting each new member, these new applicants were all taken on, en bloc and in good faith.

As it turned out, this group with the connivance of a handful of existing Chamber members would literally hijack the Chamber at the AGM. I was not re-elected nor were any of the senior officers. The unknown young Turks took on a progressive movement for which they had no experience and could get no support. On the Monday morning following the meeting, I communicated the news of its outcome to government, informing them that the entire old management committee had been wiped out.

Officials wanted to have nothing to do with untried hands without a track record. Months later the organisation was disbanded, having lost credibility and the support of its many sponsors. The new officers, on discovering the error of their ways, had the nerve to extend an invitation to me to return to lead the organisation — an invitation I rejected outright.

It was one of the saddest days of my life to see an element of community progress so painstakingly built over decades and that offered so much hope destroyed by the whims of a mindless few. But all was not lost. The initiative was resurrected and became the North London Business Development Agency, which I had the privilege to lead. I will in a new chapter show how the initiative was taken forward.

The Private Sector

By the early eighties, my company had become a reference point of black enterprise achievement in Britain — a fact recognised by 'Business in the Community', the body representing the captains of industry. An invitation to join them and my subsequent membership in its Governing Council, presided over by H.R.H. the Prince of Wales, was a signal honour. It was a significant career turning point, achieved with a not insignificant membership discount off the annual fees of £5,000 per annum.

Operating at this level I had many opportunities for speaking on a one-to-one basis with decision makers such as chief executives and chairmen of major companies and leaders of industry and commerce who were also members of the Council. Attendance at the Council's many meetings afforded me the opportunity to voice ethnic issues, sometimes publicly and at others privately, which helped to facilitate debate on issues that would otherwise not have been aired.

Debating diversity, the problems of youth and tackling inner-city blight were among the issues that good corporate citizenship called for. It was for me a great privilege to share in these very worthy causes in an area in which I was quite knowledgeable, having gained much experience over the years.

It was evident that the group valued my input in this very deserving area of need, for it led to further invitations to serve in organisations dedicated to work for improving the fabric of society. These included membership of such bodies as Race for Opportunity, another group of large companies that saw the need to place emphasis on training and the promotion of young adults in the preparation for future management roles.

The Prince's Youth Business Trust (eastern region) of which I became a director, performed a similar function with young people in business start-up and career development. The following handwritten short note from Prince Charles expresses his appreciation for my work with the Trust.

I am most appreciative of all your efforts and enthusiasm throughout 1996. This comes with my warmest best wishes for Christmas and the New Year.

Charles

The same community involvement theme used by Business in the Community, was reinforced by the Department of Trade and Industry when, in 1985, I was chosen to feature in an audio-visual case study for the British Overseas Trade Board's presentation of a short film titled '*The World is your Market*' at an export marketing conference held at the Barbican on November 5, 6 and 7 of that year. It aimed at encouraging more British companies to enter the export market.

This was a historical event and truly a high point in my career. It was a first, for a wholly black-owned company to be profiled showing the way to tackle exporting in the national drive to improve the country's export earnings. Ian Griffith, Director of Marketing at the Institute of Marketing, presented the slot 'Selecting and investigating a market' and my part in the presentation lasted a full 40 minutes.

In much the same context as '*The World is your Market*' it has been great to have my views quoted in the publication '*Working for Export Customers*' of November 1986, on the subject of exporting. The publication was written by the Confederation of British Industry

(CBI) and placed emphasis on Britain's place in the world as a trading nation.

It was a high profile publication and gave the opportunity to air my views on exporting. This was certainly gratifying and a testimony to my contribution in this field. The accolade earned me much respect within and outside the industry, as evidenced by the many comments received after the publication of the book.

In February 1984, acknowledgement of the company's achievements had come from the most eminent person in the country, the Prime Minister herself.

In a letter of January 12, her Secretary of Invitations wrote to me as follows:

'Dear Mr Wade,

The Prime Minister believes that too little attention is given to the many outstanding examples of enterprise to be found in British industry today. The reception to which you are invited is to be a celebration of that spirit of enterprise.

The Prime Minister is also aware that the success of a company depends not only on the enterprise of its founder or management, but also on the enthusiasm and loyalty of its entire workforce. She would therefore also like to invite to the reception a representative of the people working for you.

If you are able to attend the reception I should be grateful if you could write to me as soon as possible naming the person you wish to be invited from your company. I shall then be able to send an invitation to your nominee and his or her spouse.

It is usual for a press release to be issued to both the regional and national press, informing them of your attendance at the reception and giving a brief description of your company. Should you accept this invitation, the

115

Department of Trade and Industry will contact you to agree on an appropriate text but could you perhaps indicate at this stage if you would rather receive no publicity.'

February 16, the date of the reception was soon upon us. Included in my party were my wife Roslyn, my secretary Mrs Pearl Goodridge, and her husband, the Reverend Martin Goodridge. It was a very humbling experience to be one of 37 companies to have been so honoured that evening. It was, I must concede, yet another of the high points in my career to have my efforts appreciated in this way.

On my secretary's advice, a gift of the company's prized cocoa butter creams and lotions was taken to Number Ten for the Prime Minister, as an example of the kinds of products we manufactured and exported. Her letter of thanks dated February 21 stated: 'I am delighted to accept your marvellous beauty products and do hope you enjoyed the reception here.'

Our respective views on enterprise were a mutually accepted fact and I guess that in some small measure, my invitation represented in part an example of the enterprise culture that meant so much to the Prime Minister. On the whole I must have been doing something of which she approved, for I was invited back again on December 1, 1986 to one of her Christmas parties — a great honour from a lady whose leadership was an agreeable inspiration.

Career milestones in the eighties are noteworthy and have added a wonderfully rewarding dimension to my life in service to others. Simply put, it was the privilege of serving that gave me a certain joy in sharing my gifts with others.

Board of Directors of the NLBDA

Dr. Seray-Wurie
Vice-Chairman

Paul F. Creavin
Company Secretary; NatWest Bank

A.E.S. Wade
MBE, Chairman

George Martin
Vice-Chairman

Cllr. Ken Hanson
L.B. Hackney

Steve Pike
Home Office

Patich Tonge

Robin Williams
NatWest Bank

Bernadette Ijeh

E.H Cotter
Executive Director

Staff and Trainees

117

New Businesses and Community Involvement

The politics of neglect gave rise to new businesses. It was neglect that was the incubator for the Brixton Riots which flared up in 1981. These were accompanied by violence and destruction not see before in a place often described as the 'Front Line' or the 'Black capital of London' – a term that was quite apt as the earlient waves of migrants had settled in Brixton.

After being appointed by the government to lead one of the proposed initiatives to address this widespread disaffection, I named my vehicle for change The North London Business Development Agency (NLBDA). I eventually became Chairman of the organization and served for twelve years implementing the recommendations made by Lord Scarman, the judge who headed the enquiry into the riots.

The riots grew directly out of the hopelessness felt by sections of the black community at the time. Work at the grassroots within the community gave me an intimate working knowledge of the frustration felt and I was part of a group that had warned of the likely consequences if such matters were not addressed.

The Conservative Government of the day under Prime Minister Margaret Thatcher acted on Lord Scarman's report.

Central to Lord Scarman's recommendations was the need to empower ethnic peoples to become stakeholders in the economic life of the nation. NLBDA's brief was to help in facilitating this process by the provision of the following services: consultancy and advice; identifying access to finance; monitoring; providing help in locating premises; and carrying out tailor-made training programmes.

The initiative covered two London Boroughs, namely, Hackney and Haringey. After extensive discussions with various stakeholders, the project was finally kick-started by bringing on board Robin

Williams, on secondment from the National Westminster Bank, to work with me in pulling the project together. Robin's secondment was for a period of three years as part of the bank's corporate responsibility in the inner cities. His work with the agency was of the very highest quality.

We started on the project over a working lunch in the basement of the Brewery in City Road, East London, where together we hammered out our road map. First agenda items included such things as finding an office from which to operate and the appointment of a chief executive officer to manage daily affairs of the agency.

After extensive interviewing, a successful candidate was eventually found in the person of Winston Collymore. Winston had worked in local government and brought to the table skills that were beneficial in a number of ways especially in sourcing and matching project funding. His contribution in the setting goals served the agency well.

Our corporate sponsors were all well-known names in the city and included Allied Lyons PLC, Barclays Bank PLC, National Westminster Bank PLC, the Department of Employment, the Department of the Environment, my own company Dyke & Dryden Ltd, London Borough of Hackney, London Borough of Haringey, the Home Office, Shell (UK) Ltd. and the Tudor Trust.

This list was a formidable evidence of outstanding support. Their representatives were members of the Board that developed policy and oversaw the project. Over the years, I got to know these people well and remain grateful for the loyal support given me during my 12 years as Chairman.

The official opening of the agency on September 17, 1986 was a regal affair graced by Her Royal Highness, the Princess Anne. Setting the tone for the day rested to a large extent on my opening remarks as Chairman and the following is the text of what I had to say:

> 'Your Royal Highness, your Worships, Honourable gentlemen, distinguished guests, ladies and gentlemen-
> -on behalf of my Board of Directors, our Chief Executive and his team, it is my privilege to extend our warmest welcome.
>
> I would like especially to let Her Royal Highness know how delighted we are that she has chosen to honour

our agency with her presence at its official opening. Your presence here today, Your Highness, not only is an endorsement of the work we have undertaken, but also emphasizes your care and concern for the problems within the community.

I extend also our special acknowledgement to the Mayors of Hackney and Haringey, Councillor Jim Holland and Councillor Andreas Mikkides, whose councils are sponsors of the agency, and who I know share with me the satisfaction of seeing the project become a reality.

The idea of this bold and imaginative step germinated somewhere within the walls of the Home Office, represented today by the Right Honourable David Waddington, Home Office Minster of State. The community welcomes this initiative and sees it as a step in the right direction. We look forward to the Government's ongoing support for the project, which holds out great hope for the future of the local economy.

At this point, I would also like to express our thanks to the Department of the Environment for their grant assistance to the agency. Good ideas and good intentions need to be supported, by know-how, and by means of delivery and I am pleased to tell you that such support has come from some of our most distinguished companies in the private sector. Among these is the National Westminster Bank, represented by its Chairman Lord Boardman. We would like you to know just how greatly the community values the Bank's contribution.

Sponsorship has also come from Allied Lyons Plc, represented by Mr. E.B. Colwell, its Managing Director, and Shell UK Ltd by Mr Barry Dugdale, its Manager of Community Relations. Gentlemen, kindly convey our sincere thanks to your respective boards.

New Businesses and Community Involvement

Your Royal Highness, ladies and gentlemen, it would be true to say that what has evolved here is a "partnership" shaped and structured by groupings of people in a way that is novel and unique. Credit for bringing these groups together goes to Business in the Community and their Regional Director, Mr John Hyatt, who carried out most of the spadework. We offer John our thanks and remain indebted to all our supporters.

Today truly represents a landmark, and I will now ask Her Royal Highness, to proceed with the formal opening of the agency.'

After performing the ceremony of unveiling the agency's plaque, I had the great honour of being host to the Princess and showing her some examples of the many projects that we had undertaken. She showed a lively interest in what was happening, expressed her appreciation and wished the agency well in the work it had undertaken.

My first year in office tested my communication skills to the fullest in dealing with the problems inherent in reconciling working relationships in the public sector, from different disciplines and cultures. There were times at board meetings when it was extremely difficult to maintain order when tempers boiled over. It called for a special kind of skill and tact to reconcile these differences and keep members eyes on the ball.

Despite some testing times during my first year in office, I felt confident enough to deliver in my Chairman's Report the following statement.

Settling into our patch on the enterprise landscape has been for us in many ways like being put through an obstacle course. It is, no doubt, a test of our will right from the start.

In particular, bureaucratic indifference and petty political intrigue can so easily destroy the very spirit of enterprise. Fortunately, nothing was allowed to deflect me from the task and objective to which the agency

121

was committed. The NLBDA was a unique, challenging and exciting experiment for central government, local government, the private sector and the ethnic community.

Before moving on, I would in the first place like to put on record the agency's thanks to Dr Gordon Thomas who, through the Home Office, spent many long hours with Businesses in the Community, and with civic and ethnic community groups putting together the framework through which the agency was supported.

We also owe a debt of gratitude to all our sponsors who are making a most valuable contribution to the work of the agency. I am obliged to acknowledge the very special role played by our consultant, Mr Robin Williams, seconded from the National Westminster Bank which has also provided us with a quite substantial temporary loan to see us through a rather difficult period.

It is now one year on, and we can look back with great satisfaction and report that we are positively on course in responding to some local needs and meeting some of the objectives we had set ourselves. Our casework and progress in the report will readily show the exceedingly high demand that exists for our services within the local community for those either wanting to start or improve their businesses. There is indeed no better way of reducing unemployment and improving the quality of life in the neighbourhood.

The need for substantial investment in the deprived neighbourhood of Finsbury Park stared us in the face. There is urgency for the provision of managed workshop spaces, there is also a need for retraining centres, and for a revolving fund to speed up the process of regeneration of the area. There was also clear and unmistakeable evidence by the number of self-help projects initiated by various groups, of a good racial mix in the area.

As we enter our second year with the parameters firmly in place, richer by far for the experience gleaned from our past and driven by a solid commitment, we appeal to our existing and new sponsors for their continued support in helping to make Finsbury Park a happier place for all its inhabitants.

It is well worth mentioning that, while our partnership efforts have been targeted at the African and Caribbean Community, our services are equally available to all sectors of the wider community and we want to make it equally known that we have been successful in meeting this part of our remit.

I would now like to express my sincere thanks and gratitude on behalf of the African and Caribbean Community to central and local government, the private sector, and our many sponsors who have identified the business needs of the community and have generously contributed both time and money, without which our agency would not have been founded.

Finally, I would like to express my sincere thanks to my colleagues, our executive director and his team for their very gallant efforts during the past year.

With the foundations of the organisation firmly established in year one, we moved from crawling to walking, for by the end of year two, we had helped in setting up 87 new businesses that created 210 new jobs with a potential for growth and further employment. With tangible proof of our ability to deliver, additional staff was brought on board to meet the demand for the agency's services. Our case work was increasing on the basis of recommendations only that emphasises how well the service had gone down with our clients.

The early impact of the agency's success was not only showing a positive influence on the local community, but was also attracting officials from as far away as Moscow to come to observe our methods of doing things which they hoped they might use in developing small-business programmes in their own country.

A change in management welcomed the appointment of Hercules Emmanuel Cotter who assumed the role of Chief Executive. 'Manny' as he is affectionately known, brought to the table a wealth of experience gained during his study of economic development in the United States and as Principal Economic and Employment Officer for the London Borough of Hackney. His qualifications equipped him well to take on board the challenges set by our sponsors to deliver the agency's objectives.

He was visionary and blessed with the gift of gentle persuasion. Through his initiatives, he was soon to set the agency on a winning path with his rigorous and decisive approach to the job. He was the source of inspiration that led directly to the build up of 2,212 new businesses in the community during his tenure. His innovative projects included an Agency Revolving Loan Fund and the Enterprise and Management Workshop in Hackney that provided work spaces for budding entrepreneurs.

He commissioned and implemented the first specifically developed training programme for the development of staff working in enterprise agencies. Another first was the agency's thrust in bridge-building across the Atlantic allowing many of its clients to share experiences and build trading partnerships with US businesses. These facts are merely a few of the things that made NLBDA a leader in the field of enterprise development in North London.

A high point in the agency's work was that, as a result of its many successes, it was able to carry on well beyond the period of three years that was the norm for similar government-supported projects. The agency's tenth year called for a fitting 'thank you' to all the many people who had made this possible.

A celebration to mark this milestone took the form of a tenth anniversary gala enterprise and excellence awards ceremony on Saturday September 7, 1996 at the London Hilton on Park Lane. Eight hundred guests from across the land and from abroad came together to celebrate and share with us what was a truly remarkable piece of work. I append below an extract from my statement that night.

'Clocking up ten years of sustained achievement in an organisation like ours does call for a celebration! Of much more importance though, was our history and the circumstances that gave rise to our existence. Ten years ago, some of us responded to a call from Sir Leon Britain, the Home Secretary, to implement some of the recommendations made in Lord Scarman's report following the Brixton riots.

Before attempting to summarise what we have achieved over these past ten productive years, perhaps it would be helpful to look back at the broad objectives we had been set. Our first task was to increase the level of preparedness for ethnic people wanting to enter business by way of advice and counselling as a first step within our local community. Secondly, we had to work with new and existing businesses and assist in finding start-up capital and guidance as appropriate. And thirdly, we were to develop working relationships with central government, local government and the private sector, to stimulate the enterprise culture and to encourage business development in general.

How have we fared over these years? Our public accountability reports have shown both measurable and quantifiable results of which we could be justly proud.

We have succeeded in translating objectives into actions, actions into facts, and facts into statistics. Our business initiatives have moved from being local to national and from national to international in our involvement on behalf of our clients. NLBDA became a recognised resource centre in our areas of work.

In all this, we are conscious that we have done little more than barely touching a tiny part of the huge task of bridging the gap of sharing in the economic life of our nation. Racial disadvantage is fuelled in the main by the level of unemployment among ethnic communities, and the only effective response is the pursuit of fair and equal opportunity if the notion of a one-nation battle is to be won.

All the evidence we have collected points to some key facts: The need for ongoing education and training in business management is of paramount importance; there is an urgency for skills development in all areas of our activity, and access to finance remains critical in moving the black community forward to enable it to be more productive and self-supportive. To fail in these will be to perpetuate poverty for generations to come.

The black community's willingness to work hard and contribute must be recognised and, to that end, under-representation of ethnic participation in national economic life, is not so much an ethnic problem alone, it is a national problem for our country as a whole.

Ethnic business development must be seen in the context of an investment in the UK's economic future, and I urge everyone in a position to contribute in taking this process forward, to do so. Partnership is a proven way of making things happen, and indeed NLBDA is itself a product of partnership that positively advances the case for partnership that equals progress.

On behalf of my Board, our executive director and staff, I offer our sincere thanks and appreciation for the formidable support we have had from all our partners and supporters over these last ten years.'

NLBDA, as already stated earlier, was one of the many Home Office initiatives that flowed from the recommendations of Lord Scarman's enquiry on the Brixton riots. The Ethnic Minorities

Business Development Team, also under the Home Office umbrella, was another initiative that sought to broaden the scope by initiating partnerships across mainstream organisations. The primary aim being 'to enhance their knowledge of ethnic minority businesses,' and accordingly to meet community needs wherever possible.

My working relationship with the Ethnic Minorities Business Development Team (EMBDT) and its mission of into the mainstream targeted a long overdue problem that struck a chord with me. There was a tendency for ethnic businesses to follow each other into the same areas of business, thus crowding out, as it were, compatriots already in those fields of business and limiting themselves to relatively poor growth potential in a relatively small market. Diversity into the mainstream was therefore an urgent necessity for community businesses to become engaged in and to pursue the wider market place in as many varied areas of business as possible.

It is clear from the Executive Summary of May 1989 that significant progress was made in a number of key areas, moving ethnic businesses 'into the mainstream' as that mainstream itself began to recognise that their labour force and markets would, in time, become dependent on this valuable resource at their disposal.

At the third Ethnic Minority Business Initiative (EMBI) conference on November 26, 1991, at which I was one of the keynote speakers, I tried to show how wearing my Training and Enterprise Council (TEC) hat, and as a body we were trying to address diversity through our various programmes. As a member of the Ethnic Minorities Business Advisory Group (EMBAG), another Home Office initiative, I made the best use of the opportunities I had to encourage programmes that were well intentioned. While unable to quantify the results of my input, I believe that my views were seriously taken notice of and included in the recommendations we made.

A Second Chance With Love

My business life was absorbing, challenging and rewarding but lacked emotional and social interaction for some time thus leaving part of me in some ways unfulfilled. An attractive American lady called Roslyn Russell was to change all that. She was endowed with a charming come–get-me personality, petite, graceful and endowed with an almost permanent smile.

Six years had rolled by since the passing of my wife and my world revolved around my job and my children and in working with others in trying to find solutions for a more equitable society.

The ethnic hair-care industry was, in a way, a springboard for economic change in some sections within black communities and opened up opportunities for me to travel to many parts of the world where these changes were taking place. It was not surprising therefore that someone within an industry dominated by ladies with whom I was constantly surrounded and communicating all year round would challenge and break down my stern male resistance to the idea of a second serious relationship.

Roslyn Russell, the marketing director of an American company based in Washington became the person to challenge my stern defences and was to eventually break them down and become the new lady in my life. Roz, as she was affectionately known to her many friends, was a high flyer in the hair-care industry.

She worked for the Hairlox company in Washington and drove the successful development of their brand known as the Capital Curl. The company took part in my first Afro Hair & Beauty exhibition at the Grosvenor House Hotel in Mayfair, London and was a key player in the presentations that took place.

It was customary for me to entertain our guests and the Capital Curl team was included in our after-the-show party. Pilgrims' Rest in Palmers Green was my favourite place for entertaining. It was while dining there that my Capital Curl guest without warning tucked into my 'steak Dianne' and helped herself.

The audacity of this intervention knocked me out for sure and with that she charmed her way into my life. My resistance was broken. Whether we had anything in common was still to be tested and would take time to discover. There was of course a shared common interest in the industry and especially being competitors we had lots to talk about.

A fondness grew over months and so too did the appearance that we were major shareholders in our respective telephone companies as evidenced by the quarterly telephone bills on both sides of the Atlantic. Of major concern to me in this equation was my friendship with Marcus Griffith, her boss, the owner of the Hairlox company. The possibility of his losing to me a key member of his staff bothered me greatly.

The honourable thing to do was to talk things over with the professor, as Marcus was known, and seek his valuable advice on the subject. In the first place he let it be known that to best of his knowledge I was talking with a decent and much respected lady. On the question of the possible loss of a greatly valued member of his team, he reasoned that her personal happiness would mean much more to her than staying on with his company. With that said, it was now up to me to take a decision.

Back in London I pondered long and hard over what was a really very difficult decision, taking into account the well-being and welfare of my children and how a second wife would fit with my existing family arrangements. Several round-table conversations with the children and visits by Roslyn got things going.

The year 1986 became another personal milestone that ended with my children and me winging our way to Washington DC where the wedding took place. Our respective families gave us their blessings and Roslyn accepted my children as her own as part of the ceremony. This public statement of commitment filled me with the confidence that the emotional needs of my children would be taken care of.

Her colleagues from work and her friends in Washington including the Mayor of the city, Marion Barry, all turned up to offer their good wishes. The day was not without its funny sides. One of Roz's friends was in some ways the centre of attraction. She stole what is usually the bride's show. Dressed to kill, as the saying goes, in an ensemble that emphasised the biggest derriere ever seen, she had a charming personality and poked fun at herself, declaring that walking the streets of the city she quite often held up traffic with her many admirers! 'If you have something to show', she asserted, 'why not flaunt it.'

After the reception the joke was on me. I had excused myself to visit the bathroom and quite accidentally the lock jammed with me inside. Concerned about my long absence, a search party had discreetly set out to find me. Fortunately, my call for help was heard. Outside the toilet there were fits of laughter and endless jokes about my voluntary imprisonment.

The incident became a talking point for the rest of the evening. 'Are you already running away before you've even got started?' some wanted to know.

Len Dyke, one my business colleagues who attended the wedding from the office provided yet another now famous joke that kept everyone laughing for days. With his camera cocked, he had set about taking as many photos as he could, only to discover after it all that there was no film in his camera! 'How stupid have I been?' he accused himself.

Back in London, Roslyn eventually joined the company wearing two hats: one covering product education and the other, promotions management. She lived up to my expectations in this dual role by broadening the scope of the company's engagement with its public in both those aspects of business.

On the education front, she communicated a better understanding of the use of chemicals and, to that end, succeeded in building our educational relationships across the industry to bring about change in product usage.

One of the most significant of these changes was her teaming up with Winston Isaccs of Splinters Academy fame on Maddox Street. Winston was the leading technician in the hair-care industry in the UK and, as such, his salon was patronised by the elite in the society. By teaming up with Splinters, between them, we became spokespersons for the company's brands, endorsing them in the best possible light. Education and promotion was the formula that made Super Curl a leading brand of its day.

Her success at what she did endeared her to a large circle of friends, especially at the Afro Hair Beauty exhibitions. It was clear from the vibes circulating after the promotions that some folks within the organisation somehow felt threatened. The trigger for this under—current came to light in an article handed to Roslyn and myself on a flight to Atlanta by Jane Hammond, the company's public relations person. It read: 'The chairman opened the event by welcoming everyone, but when Mrs Roslyn Wade, the company's "First Lady" came on stage, everyone knew exactly who was in charge.'

The journalist who wrote the article was I am sure not malicious, but the article had the effect of creating for my wife and me, what amounted to an incalculable disaster in our relationships with colleagues within the company.

On our return from our business trip, we found the air poisoned with intrigue and the type of behaviour associated with the small minds of people unsure of where they stood in the scheme of things. This destructive episode killed off what was a strategic plank patiently put together for driving the business forward by myself and Roslyn.

The subsequent behaviour of my colleagues over the incident of a mere article in the press led me to believe that the matter was orchestrated out of all proportion. Their plan was to remove my wife from the organisation in light of a perceived threat from both of us to take over the company. Over this disastrous issue, a once harmonious working relationship floundered.

Roslyn felt she could no longer work with people she could not trust and became restive, moving back and forth to the US, a situation that made life difficult for me. She tried to persuade me to sell out and move with her to the US but this was something I simply could not do. There was too much at stake in the UK.

This issue became a struggle between my heart and my head. On our return from what was a most glorious cruising holiday, we shared a number of memorable events together including my investiture at the Palace and a celebration at Number Ten as guests of the Prime Minister.

An attempt at finding a compromise to what had become a grave difficulty for us both, led to my wife's moving back to the US without me — a situation from which we did not recover. It remains, however, a chapter in my life preserved by the mutual respect and friendship we continue to have for each other.

A Day at Buckingham Palace

with
Left to right: Anthony Wade, Jnr., wife Rosalyn
and daughter Deborah

An Invitation to Buckingham Palace

Back in London the pace of engagements was much the same as before, save that the old adage held true that a change was just as good as a rest. In my in-tray was a letter from the Principal Private Secretary at 10 Downing Street dated May 1, 1987 stamped 'In confidence'. It read, 'The Prime Minister has asked me to inform you, in strict confidence, that she has in mind, on the occasion of the list of Birthday Honours, to submit your name to the Queen with a recommendation that Her Majesty may be graciously pleased to approve that you be appointed a Member of the Order of the British Empire.'

It went on, 'Before doing so, the Prime Minister would be glad to be assured that this would be agreeable to you. I should be grateful if you would let me know by completing the enclosed form and sending it back to me by return of post.' I duly dispatched my acceptance and waited to hear further keeping faith with the request for confidence.

Later, a further letter arrived from the Central Chancery Of the Orders Of Knighthood dated September 22, which gave details of the date and time of the investiture, set for December 15, 1987. The date finally arrived and my family and I were on our way to the Palace.

After being admitted, we attended a briefing that detailed the rules of protocol, which were to be followed to the letter. Roslyn, Deborah and Tony Junior were led to the visitors' gallery, to a vantage point from which to observe the ceremony, while I was escorted to the receiving gate to listen for my name to be called. This was not an everyday affair, and a state of controlled nervousness, somehow disguised, prevailed until the moment I heard my name. In the moments that followed, a muffled calm came over me as I strode to the podium to be decorated.

Her Majesty's smile and her kind words soothed away the tension as she pinned the medal on my lapel. She had obviously been briefed about my work, for she wanted to know if I was enjoying it. Very much I responded. I fought hard to remember the last words of my briefing, 'you are never to turn your back on the Queen, move two steps backwards and then take a right turn, and that leads the way out from the ceremony'. I was relieved that I followed the briefings correctly.

The event remains for me a moment of great honour. The citation was for my contribution to employment. It was with a sense of much humility that I offered my sincere thanks to my staff and all the people who had made that occasion possible. Following the ceremony and for days later, it was heart-warming the number of messages of congratulation that came from a wide cross-section of society. It was a really comforting feeling to discover that I had so many friends.

Later that day, a private party for relations and friends rounded off what was a fitting end to a memorable day. Months later, a public party acknowledging the honour was organised by the community, whose members were, in my judgement, the true recipients, while I was simply the agent.

In their
footsteps

A tribute to the pioneers and innovators
of the Black beauty industry

The Board of Directors
for the year ended 31 March 1995

John Wilkinson
Chairman - Retired
ESAB Group UK Ltd
NLTEC Chairman
Retired 30.11.94

Steve Clayton
Managing Director
Leaside Buses
NLTEC Chairman
Appointed 1.12.94

Mike Nixon
NLTEC Chief Executive

John Bathe
Financial Secretary
Graphical Paper and
Media Union (GPMU)
NLTEC Board Director

Trevor Berry
Regional Managing Director
John Laing Construction Ltd
NLTEC Board Director

John Clayton
Managing Director
Newman Labelling Machines Ltd
NLTEC Board Director

Anthony Felix
Chairman
Chase Farms Hospitals
NHS Trust
NLTEC Board Director

Michael Gerson
Managing Director
Michael Gerson Ltd
NLTEC Board Director

Jennifer Hoyland
Principal
Hendon College
NLTEC Board Director

Peter Kerry
Regional Services Manager
British Gas Plc
NLTEC Board Director

Amobi Modu
Director
Finsbury Park Community Trust
NLTEC Board Director

Terry Schaefer
Plant Manager
Ford Motor Company Ltd
NLTEC Board Director

Gu Bux Singh
Chief Executive
London Borough of Haringey
NLTEC Board Director

Anthony Wade
Managing Director
Dyke & Dryden Ltd
NLTEC Board Director

Derek Wheeler
Manager
Marks & Spencer PLC
NLTEC Board Director

Stephen Hales
Director
Financial Insurance Group
NLTEC Company Secretary

A team with which I had the privilege to work in serving the people of Barnet, Enfield and Harringey in taking forward government policy through the Training and Enterprise Councils.

North London Training & Enterprise Council (TEC)

Training and Enterprise Councils have been among the most successful management innovations of the last decade of the twentieth century, and for me it was a great privilege to have been part of this national movement from start to finish.

I served as a Board Director for the full ten years that the project existed. My souvenir copy of the book prepared by the TEC National Council to mark the work of the movement, occupies a place of pride in my library.

Attached to my copy of the book is a copy of the minutes of our first board meeting that highlighted my nomination of Mike Nixon for the position of Chief Executive. This was endorsed and carried by the board. He served, like myself, for the full ten years of the TEC's active life and proved a worthy holder of that office.

What is a TEC? This is a question I have often been asked in conversation with visiting friends from abroad and sometimes by folks on the home front. It is an employer-led grouping of individuals with a mission to foster economic growth with ownership vested in the local community to whom the TEC is answerable.

The legal framework of the boards was made up as follows: Two thirds were drawn from the private sector at managing director or chief executive level and the other third from the public sector, trade unions and the voluntary sectors. TECs were a unique combination of cultures with one common thread running through them. The people that made up their boards were all eminently successful at what they did in their respective fields.

Since they were drawn from the local communities in which they lived and worked, their knowledge of local needs was best understood by them in almost all the areas that would make for a healthy and socially cohesive community. These included such matters as the education needs of the area, raising standards, fighting exclusion in employment, developing skills needed for a particular industry, etc.

This understanding enabled the board to tailor solutions to address particular problems.

The other element of their uniqueness was the loyal commitment undertaken by a board of volunteers of like-minded people working for the common good of the community. Our vision at NLTEC as we all saw it was the challenge, the potential, the opportunity and the solution. Each of our directors was required to give a short summary of his/her perspective for a give-away of the TEC vision. The following was what I had to say:

> 'I believe that the basic essentials in attaining a local industrious culture in the widest possible sense of the word are education and training, which create opportunities, that generate ideas, that lead to prosperity. My contention has always been that every local community, whatever its make-up, needs to be assertive and innovative, ensuring that its local talents and skills are put to the best possible use for the common good of the local community. I like the TEC concept for it seeks to put local people in the driving seat of the local community and its basic economic needs.'

Recapturing some aspects of those ten years fills one with a sense of pride at being able to serve in many areas that had a direct bearing on changing attitudes and putting across a community case that helped to cultivate a climate of change for the better. I will quote from a speech I made while representing our TEC at a TEC National Conference at the Queen Elizabeth II Conference Centre on November 26, 1991.

> 'Chairman, ladies and gentlemen, I bring greetings from the Board of North London TEC. I would like to take this opportunity to briefly tell you a little about some of the things we are doing at North London TEC in relation to the ethnic section of our community, and of our whole approach to the work in general. For the benefit of those who do not know our area, we cover the Boroughs of Barnet — an area of 49 square miles, Enfield — 30 square miles and Haringey — 11.7 with a population of 762,000.

North London Training and Enterprise Council (TEC)

In Haringey we share, to a large extent, many of the characteristics of the inner city, yet with marked contrasts between our eastern and western parts of the borough. The social composition in Haringey reflects a wide ethnic diversity, which includes many refugee groups. In fact, our ethnic minority community constitutes over a third of the population, that is, 63,000 out of 190,000 which leads me to tell you that the catchment area of Tottenham presents us with the most formidable challenge. Perhaps, if I may, I will just put in perspective the scale of that challenge.

Government figures show that Haringey ranks as the sixth most deprived authority in England, in the Department of the Environment's own index of urban deprivation. In a study undertaken by the Department of Education and Science, to measure educational needs, Haringey was also identified as being within the cluster demonstrating the most socio-economic disadvantage and educational need.

The question you may well ask is how are we approaching this challenge? First, our mission statement is clear and positive. We aim to make North London a recognised area of opportunity for individual and corporate prosperity.

Under the distinguished leadership of our chairman Tony Felix, we have sought to ensure the involvement of our whole community, through people who have showed commitment to take on board the challenge, people who saw the potential, people who saw the opportunity, and were willing to work for a solution.

Among the specific things we have done thus far are the following: our Adult/youth training provision reflects the high priority we place on targeting our marketing and promotion activities, to ensure that participation in training programmes reflects the ethnic make-up of those within our three boroughs.

The latest national statistical returns show that the take-up rate of training places by unemployed ethnic minorities averages only 13 per cent nationally. This compares with NLTEC's 55 per cent of all trainees coming through from ethnic minorities.

Again our enterprise provision to assist self-employment shows a high percentage of ethnic minority take-up. We have advertised our new Enterprise Allowance Scheme via the ethnic language press which includes Greek, Turkish, Guguratee, Hindu and Punjabi papers.

There has been the formation of an advisory group to monitor our strategic objectives of the needs of ethnic minorities, in the areas of training, enterprise and education. Advisory group membership comprises educationalists, representation of voluntary and ethnic groups. This group will build on the earlier work undertaken by our Task groups, which resulted in the production of a report that was used to write up our corporate plan.

Our TEC has positively reacted to the newly launched Ethnic Minorities Group (EMG), and has worked in partnership with local authorities and representatives of voluntary groups to ensure that every possible assistance is given to develop proposals for submission. The TEC has submitted 15 such proposals on behalf of Kurds, Somali, Eretrians, Tamils, Greek, Turks, and groups representing others from Central Africa.

In summary, Chairman, in all that I have said, it was

our boards' intention to give ownership and enrichment to the lives of all the people of Barnet, Enfield and Haringey.'

It was not by any stretch of the imagination easy going. TEC work had to be fitted in with my day job running of my company. Surrounding oneself with able people and the ability to delegate is the secret in getting things done. Key assignments at NLTEC included board membership and Deputy Chairman of the Enterprise Committee and the Enterprise Club, a grouping of companies from within our three Boroughs which numbered some 750 members. These were important assignments in which one was contributing and learning at the same time, and to have been delegated to lead these groups was, in a way, testimony to my commitment to service in these areas.

I believe I can make some modest claim to having plotted many aspects of my journey with a deep sense of pride. One such aspect in particular was the invitation for me to serve as a member of the Corporation of the College of North East London as the TEC's board representative.

As an old boy of the college, I felt a particular element of satisfaction in being able to contribute and give something back by being part of the governing body dealing with policy direction and funding of the TEC and allowing it to fulfil its education remit for the people of Barnet, Enfield and Haringey.

In concluding this part of my journey, Mike Nixon's summary in a book marking TECs ten years of TECs/CCTEs, captures brilliantly what transpired during those years and speaks for the entire board:

'The North London Training & Enterprise council (NLTEC) has successfully served the London Boroughs of Barnet, Enfield and Haringey since its launch in September 1991. Frequently judged the best performing TEC in London and among the best in England and Wales, NLTEC has developed numerous practical partnerships from which tens of thousands of local people and businesses have benefited. The North London Training & Enterprise Council is proud of its exceptional record of delivery and the strength of its partnerships. We leave a legacy of strong sustainable partnerships capable of increasing employment and learning opportunities for local people and growth for local businesses. These partnerships will form a powerful launching pad on which successive bodies may build.'

THE college OF NORTH EAST LONDON

From: Tony Corder, Chair of the Corporation

Principal: Ian Macwhinnie
Tel: 0181 802 3111
Fax: 0181 442 3091
☐ Bounds Green Centre, Park Road, London N11 2OF.
☐ Muswell Hill Centre, Rhodes Avenue, London N22 4UT.
☐ Tottenham Centre, High Road, London N15 4RU.

Tony Wade Esq
19 Bernard Road
London N15 4NE

Dear Tony,

23rd January.

I am writing on behalf of the Corporation to record our appreciation of the services you have given to the College as a Member of the Governing Body. It was with great regret that we learnt of you resignation but remain very grateful to you for your time and considered contribution you were able to offer in a very busy schedule.

For my own part I have valued highly the wit and wisdom you have brought to our deliberations. Thank you.

I hope you are now enjoying better health. I also hope that our paths may cross again at some stage in the future.

With every good wish

Yours sincerely

Tony Corder

Tony Corder

Other Centres

Tetherdown Centre
Tetherdown,
London N10 1ND
0181 883 9241

Tottenham Green Centre
Town Hall Approach Rd
London N15 4RX
0181 802 3111

Falkland Centre
Falkland Road,
London N8 0NU
0181 348 3028

Adult Reading Centre
Mattison Road,
London N4 1BD
0181 348 6600

143

A Merger that went Wrong

Life's journey has its high and low points and comes to us all in different ways. Among the lows I have had to live with for a time was the sale of two-thirds of my company to Soft Sheen Industries.

It was not that I was forced to sell. I acted of my own free will and was instrumental in taking the sale process forward from our side of the fence. It was, as a matter of fact, a deliberate act to opt to sell to Soft Sheen, a company I respected for what it had achieved and had done for the black community in Chicago. I really thought that our philosophies were similar and that we could work together.

At the time there were other serious offers for the company and one in particular from TCB, (which incidentally stands for taking care of business) owned by the American multinational, Alberta Culver. TCB was desperate to buy Dyke & Dryden once news of the sale leaked out. Mr Dan Lewis, a senior vice-president of TCB, whom I got to know well, visited my office twice, arriving from the US by private jet in a bid to cut a deal.

His plan, he explained, was that as his corporation had already taken a decision to expand their huge Sally Stores retail chain into the UK, he would be willing to pay over and above anything that Soft Sheen offered for the business. 'Your stores would fit nicely into our plans' he insisted. It was a done deal with Soft Sheen, I told him, in an effort to remove the pressure he was exerting on me to swing things his way.

The truth was that, keen as I was to play a part in helping to build a credible black business structure across the Atlantic, as important as money was, it was really a secondary consideration as far as I was concerned.

The spirit of Marcus Mosiah Garvey was moving within me, and I quote him. 'You will see from the start we tried to dignify our race.' With Soft Sheen as the largest player in our industry in the United States and Dyke & Dryden in the same position in the UK, I had a vision that, between us, our stated objective was possible. I thought joining forces would help to dignify the black business community. Dan Lewis nevertheless succeeded in carrying out his plans by buying Ogee Ltd, a white-owned company that was in the salon distribution business, but primarily in the general market sector.

The sale of Dyke & Dryden came about at the time it did because my colleagues, Len and Dudley, indicated to me in 1986 that they wished to sell their shares in the company. The companies' articles gave me first option to buy, and while pondering their proposal during a visit to Nigeria, I ran into Gary Gardener, then President of Soft Sheen. As it happened he was on a similar mission as I was, seeking to consolidate our respective positions in that market.

Gary had earlier expressed his interest in purchasing my company if my partners and I were ever to consider selling. I let it be known that my colleagues had decided to sell and this was now his opportunity. He reaffirmed his interest, and we both called it a deal, provided that I was prepared to stay with the company. I confirmed that it was my intention so to do and we shook hands on a deal in principle. On my return to London, I conveyed the news to my colleagues who were receptive. The next step was to place matters in the hands of our respective lawyers and have our accountants sort out the paperwork. It was a full year before completion of sale in October 1987.

News of the sale having been released at a press conference brought a mixed reception from the black community in Britain. Some objected to the sale, arguing that it denied British blacks the pride of ownership they shared and wished it had gone to people within the black community in Britain. Others cited the economy of scale and welcomed it as a first in black transatlantic partnership and a positive pointer in black business development.

Black Beauty Professional, a weighty quarterly trade publication, following the acquisition came out with an article headlined, 'A hair raiser.' The article read:

> 'When the dust finally settles over this quarter's main news story regarding the acquisition of a major stake in Dyke & Dryden by Soft Sheen Industries Ltd, the Ethnic Health & Beauty Aids sector will have time to reflect on what this take-over means for the industry as a whole.
>
> As the country's leading distributor of black hair and skin-care products, Dyke & Dryden had established for

itself, over the years, a more or less unrivalled position, but this might now come under threat following the Soft Sheen Merger. Other manufacturers may not be too keen to offer their products to Dyke & Dryden for distribution as they view this as an indirect way of propping up two competing manufacturers.

Dyke & Dryden's Super Curl and Natural Beauty ranges, now coupled with Soft Sheen's Carefree Curl and Optimum retail and professional ranges, will make the "New" Dyke & Dryden into a significant manufacturing force. Soft Sheen, although enjoying good distribution at present, has nonetheless suffered from severe stock shortages in the past and, by now having a fixed presence in the UK, its stock position should improve significantly.

Equally, Super Curl/Natural Beauty may now be able to make a serious attempt to break into the US market, which in the past has been difficult. Now under Soft Sheen's wing the British black hair and skin-care lines could enjoy lucrative US sales.'

One industry observer highlighted a point to ponder: 'Mergers usually take place either to strengthen your position in the market place or to stop further decline. What was the reason behind this particular merger? Only time will tell.'

The low point career-wise to which I referred earlier was the unfulfilled vision as well as the broken solemn promises made by the principals of Soft Sheen's stated objectives. The press statements by Edward Gardener, Chairman and Gary Gardener, President of Soft Sheen were abundantly clear.

'This merger is exciting and historical from two perspectives,' said Gary. 'We have a tendency as black business people of not coming together.' He continued: 'There are 23,000,000 black people in the United States and 320,000,000 around the world. Like the British did several hundred years ago, we have to get out of this little island.'

Chairman Edward Gardener was equally clear. 'The expansion into the UK with Dyke & Dryden, a firm whose philosophy is very close to ours, is exciting. It is only proper that we join hands and create a stronger organization so that we can do more for our communities.' The above quotes are from the *Chicago Chatham-Southeast – Citizen*, February 5, 1988.

In my statement, I concurred with those already made by my new business partners, adding that hopefully it made good business sense to join forces with the Soft Sheen group of companies, a group several times larger than we were and whose expressed commitment was to repeat in the UK, Europe and Africa what they had done in the United States.

In Dyke & Dryden's press release of October 1988, I indicated that I had no reason to doubt the undertakings given by Soft Sheen, and believed that the controlling interest they had bought represented a turning point in the history of black businesses working together across the Atlantic.

Hardly had the ink of the optimistic expressions by the Gardeners and myself dried on the paper than Soft Sheen's staff in Chicago made what was the most elementary mistake that a company could ever make. They played right into the hands of their competition by releasing the following statement:

'By buying into Europe's largest distributor, we have stolen a march on our competition, profiting from them through our subsidiary' they gloated. This was a colossal error of judgement, seeing that the distribution side of Dyke & Dryden's business depended to a large extent on supplies coming from their competition. That was the first serious mistake, but worse was yet to come.

The response to that inept statement was immediate and severe. Our once good friends refused to continue to supply us, finding a thousand and one excuses not to do so, and opened up new distributors around us. The immediate effect on Dyke & Dryden was a loss of sales from many of our once loyal customers that soon began to hurt. In the meantime, the market was watching and waiting to see what would be the response from the big brother who now controlled the show.

In developing the master plan during the sale and purchase negotiations, I was mindful of the objectives that coloured Gary's thinking. He had set his sights on the size of the market that lay within his grasp, taking into account our penetration into the huge African market. Added to Soft Sheen's manufacturing capability and technical know-how and Dyke & Dryden's distribution network, it all seemed on face value the perfect marriage.

The first step in the grand design was to use the Dyke & Dryden distribution network to dominate the market across Europe and Africa; secondly, to expand the retail chain in the UK; and thirdly, to build the Super Curl and Natural Beauty brands. This also included a proposal to buy one of our suppliers, DHL Products, a company in Bradford, England that was currently manufacturing most of our brands. In that connection, formulas were despatched from the US and everything seemed to be on a roll.

On paper, these visionary aspirations were wonderful, but putting them into practice was a totally different ball game. In the preparation for take-off, it was agreed that it made good sense to harmonize the companies' computer systems, taking into account the many benefits that linking up would bring to the organization. In December 1987, my finance director, Kingsley Peter and I visited Chicago for a meeting with our opposite numbers in an effort to pull our synergies together.

Our first disagreement occurred over the purchase of a new compatible computer system for Dyke & Dryden. Our view was that the purchase should be made in the UK, so that if for no other reason, we would have easy access to the servicing arrangements that would be required from time to time.

The Americans on the other hand differed and displayed a strong attitude of 'we know best'. They lacked good manners and I made a mental note at the time that with that attitude it was going to be difficult working with them. We eventually arrived at a compromise by buying the hardware in the UK and the software in the US. That meeting brought home to me for the time in no uncertain way, the loss of my executive decision making role.

As Kingsley and I predicted, accessing and trying to technically service the system from thousands of miles away by telephone was idiotic and resulted in costs to us in the order of approximately £100,000, money we could ill afford. Kingsley's frustration boiled over on this and several other management issues and forced him to resign his position with the company. This bungling had cost Dyke & Dryden its most senior manager and valuable staff member.

Recruiting a replacement locally in the UK presented yet another problem. Someone who had worked closely with the President and Vice President of Finance was transferred to London at considerable cost. The living expenses had to be met by Dyke & Dryden. I reasoned, however, that with someone in whom they both had confidence perhaps this should make transparency and all related matters palatable, therefore I agreed with the secondment but with hindsight, it would not have made any difference whether I did or not.

The difficulty was that the person on secondment was clearly not given the wherewithal to do the job. What was required was access to stock to meet the massive shortages in the market for certain Soft Sheen brands to generate cash to stop the business bleeding to death following the refusal by other companies to supply Dyke & Dryden after the profiteering gaffe made by Soft Sheen's personnel.

Shortages of Soft Sheen brands in the market got even worse despite the fact that they were now the majority owners of the company. It was the first fulfillment of the analysis by the 'hair raiser' article. The person seconded had no clout and was letting down D&D by her inability to speak up. Reports to Chicago were misleading and failed to give a fair and true picture of the situation as it existed.

My position as Managing Director remained unchanged but this was in name only, for all the decisions were now being taken in Chicago. Notwithstanding, within the company the staff looked to me for solutions. Under this daily pressure I never lost my nerve. I knew I could not and somehow found a reserve of inner strength which situations like these call for.

Our bank with whom I had worked for many years and remained on good terms was willing to provide the funds we required, provided that our new parent company was willing to put up the required guarantee. Mick Leonard, my relationship manager at Barclays, could not have been more helpful. At his own expense he accompanied me to Chicago and laid his cards on the table showing that he was willing to provide the working capital the company required. He, however, insisted that he must have Soft Sheen's signature on the dotted line now that the company was American controlled.

Soft Sheen was either not prepared or was unable to sign, arguing that the assets held by the bank more than covered the borrowings. This did not meet with the bank's calculation of the figures, which they discounted drastically and stuck to their guns. On the basis of my track record with the bank they were willing to stand behind the company, but as a minority shareholder, I was left hurting in the tussle. I was advised that it was dangerously unwise to put up the guarantee for the majority shareholder considering the dangers to which I was now exposed.

Barclays had had enough of playing games with Soft Sheen and acted by directing a letter to me as Managing Director, setting out their new lending terms to the company and reducing the company's overdraft facility from £275,000 by an initial £100,000, and thereafter in chunks of £50,000 a time, down to the level of a mere £15,000. Despite this drastic move, Chicago still did not budge and the crisis deepened.

What transpired amounted to a callous indifference and cruel exploitation of the generosity and goodwill of the shareholder who had already sold his shares in the business cheaply by flatly refusing larger sums from other interested purchasers, all in the name of strengthening and encouraging black commercial solidarity across the black diaspora. This for me was agony.

The stalemate dragged on and the crisis deepened, but still there was no action on the part of Soft Sheen in the crisis and matters were allowed to drift further. The distress thus caused within the organization was incalculable. Staff drifted away and the hardships for the company increased to the point where we were now dangerously on the verge of going under.

Eventually, an independent enquiry was called for and carried out by Stoy-Hayward, one of the four big accounting firms in the country. Their findings were as follows: 'It is our impression that the position of the Managing Director has been obscured by the involvement of Soft Sheen personnel in the day-to-day management of the business.

Overall responsibility for decision making, no longer appears to be vested in Tony Wade, the Managing Director, but to be diffused between Soft Sheen personnel working at the company. The result is that the company lacks clear direction, and all decision making is a protracted and inconclusive process.'

The clarity of the independent findings by Stoy–Hayward, explains what was an ongoing, impossible and frustrating daily situation in dealing with Soft Sheen's personnel in Chicago. Staff at Dyke & Dryden who were with me from the beginning became demoralized. Some left the company, while others hung on in the vain hope that things would get better. But they did not. I found it difficult to understand why a company would make an investment of hundreds of thousands of pounds and sit by and watch it go to waste.

A Merger that went Wrong

Quite clearly, something of which I had no knowledge had gone seriously wrong within Soft Sheen's core management circle. Gary Gardener, the President with whom I had done the deal in good faith, was by then refusing to take my calls—the mystery deepened.

Months later I was to learn that Gary as President and his wife as Vice President of Marketing were no longer with the company. Events to follow were left to speculation. The reality of the possibility of bankruptcy stared me in the face if Soft Sheen continued to have anything to do with the business.

My only recourse was to offer to buy back the business and capitalize on the goodwill and the not insignificant assets that still existed in freehold properties, leaseholds, valuable trademarks and stocks that were all the results of my hard work in the first place. Faced with this predicament I had no choice but to act, proving for a second time that conviction, dedication and a sense of purpose are the essential drivers of success. I acted on my conviction and bought my company back.

Defeating the 'Young Turks'

In the face of this unbelievable turmoil, a formal offer to buy the company back was made to Soft Sheen through my solicitors in February 1994. The offer was at first rejected. However, in September the following year, a deal was struck and the company reverted to me including the subsidiary, Afro Hair & Beauty Ltd.

The re-acquisition of the company had not been achieved without a battle to ward off the ambitions of my senior managers who, without my knowledge, had put in a bid to Soft Sheen to buy their interest in the company. This was a move planned in collusion with some senior Soft Sheen personnel. It was a witless move, for it could only succeed with my agreement. Unknown to the 'Young Turks,' built into my contract was a card I had up my sleeve.

Unflappability was one of my many strengths and I knew instinctively when to call the bluff of my conspirators, put them through the wringer and hang them out to dry at the appropriate time. The services of these managers were humanely dispensed with in a timely manner by playing them at their own game, appearing to go along with their proposal and at the right and least expected moment turning the tables on them.

Sure enough, they too were victims of blunders that had originated in Chicago and had also to endure the agony and hardships imposed on us by Soft Sheen. But to try to relieve me of my investment in the manner in which they attempted lacked decency and was riddled with collusion. The confidence I had had in them went out the window and it was a matter of outsmarting them. I did and I felt really good about it!

The truth was that following the acquisition of the majority shareholding in Dyke & Dryden, the company's position was undermined firstly by the utterances of Soft Sheen's personnel themselves as already stated. Secondly, they were clearly unable to deliver on the promises they had made and it is not difficult to speculate on the reasons why. Observers of the scene wanted to know if due diligence had been carried out, to which the short answer was yes. Unfortunately our bank manager and accountants had sight only of turnover figures that did not reveal the whole story behind the gloss on the company.

With the business now back in my hands, it was in many respects a question of literally starting all over again. The power of positive thinking and my father's dictum were for me always a major strength, and really nothing less could have prepared me mentally for the mammoth task that lay ahead in rebuilding the business. I told myself I had done it once and could do it again. And I did.

Confident in this belief, I rigged a restructuring plan. It entailed getting right back, as it were, to basics, stripping the organization of all its unproductive elements. With decision making now back where it belonged, I had no one to answer to about how to use my pruning knife.

Ruthlessness was never part of my make-up, but in the circumstances that prevailed, it was the only course of action that I could follow to restore the dignity and respectability of a proud organisation. By being too trusting in the beginning with Soft Sheen, I had allowed them to get off on the cheap in preference to taking TCB's superior offer. I was made to suffer as a result—a bitter pill for me to swallow.

Getting staff numbers down to as few as possible was a first step, followed by lopping off the retail segment of the company. Some units were sold appropriately to members of staff on easy terms, while others were sold to outsiders. The final unit to be sold was the retail flagship store in the Wood Green Shopping City complex.

Trying to broker a deal with my landlord in giving up my flagship store on which there was a twenty-five-year lease was like playing on a sticky wicket. News was leaked to me about plans to revamp sections of the complex that included my unit. Unwittingly, I revealed the sale of the unit and they found every excuse not to grant a licence to several prospective purchasers for it. In the end it became cheaper to pay them for the ten years unexpired portion of the lease.

The wholesale and general distribution side of the business was dealt with in a similar fashion as had happened with the retail division, thus leaving the company free to focus on what was its most profitable segment, the manufacturing of its brands. The subsidiary Afro Hair & Beauty was also retained, more of which I will deal with later.

My new direction was communicated to the industry and from there on it was simply a question of managing change, driven by one objective, that of restoring the financial health and respect of the company.

The challenge was formidable, but certainly achievable as long as I stayed focussed on the goals that I had set for the organization and, to that end, a new energetic and experienced manager was hired to implement the company's new direction. A new management team was formed, led by an accountant with many years of experience in the industry who knew most of the customers well. His mastery of creative accounting and relationship management kept everyone happy until we were in a position to deal with our creditors.

The other key cog in the new team was my personal assistant and confidant, Claudia Newton, a first class all-rounder, providing me with support far beyond the call of duty. I will always be indebted to her super contribution in restoring the health and pride of the company.

Confidence returned once the industry received the news that I was back in the driver's seat. It was truly a source of great comfort to discover that my many industry friends held me in such high esteem, and for this I have been truly grateful.

Funding the turnaround was, fortunately, not too difficult a process. It simply meant turning one of the company's unencumbered freehold properties into cash and, with prudent and tight accounting policies, we were well on our way to discovering new horizons for the business.

A new and imaginative marketing campaign was launched to coincide with the 1996 Afro Hair & Beauty exhibition, with a clear and positive statement circulated to our many customers and the industry friends at home and abroad. The market response to our new vibrant colour cosmetics range designed by make-up consultants, 'the Beauty Bar', went down like a treat with the ladies of all ages and shades.

Our brands that had stood the test of time were enhanced and improved in most areas, regaining their market position. At the same time, new products were added to our ranges and new markets found overseas.

Revisiting the circumstances that gave rise to the introduction of the company's own brands are well remembered. There was a haunting vision of the need to manufacture the company's own brands to provide a measure of self-sufficiency which, in the end, became the cornerstone of the company's recovery and survival in a market that had matured with time.

Looking back, it turned out to be one of the most exhilarating times of my life, a time that infused a new spirit of adventure, a new sense of freedom and creativity which is in essence, I believe, at the heart of all achievement, turning negatives into positives.

Dyke & Dryden had many strengths and one of them was its subsidiary, Afro Hair & Beauty. A & B owned no assets, but was a brand on which Elkin Pianim, son-in-law of the media mogul Rupert Murdock, had set his sights. One day without an appointment, he arrived at my office and explained to me that the exhibition would fit nicely with the *Nation*, a newspaper business he owned. This was a very pleasant surprise, and what was even more surprising, after a relatively short debate, he made me an offer for the company that was hard to refuse.

As it seemed that everything was for sale at the right price, there and then I did a deal with him. The deal was timely, providing an unexpected pool of cash that strengthened the new Dyke & Dryden's liquidity position and made the going less turbulent. Part of the deal included a non-executive directorship on the *Nation's* board and a salary.

Selling off A & B suited me nicely in that it removed the necessity of having to cope with the management of A & B and allowed me to focus on the development of the Dyke & Dryden brands.

The new source of funds made all the difference. It removed the dependence on bank borrowing and, combined with strong leadership, was enough to restore the company's good health and pride of place within the industry.

A new chapter in my life with
**wife Vasantha
Daughter Sarah
Grand-daughter Naomi**

Love for a Third Time

Finding myself in love for a third time at age fifty meant there must be something after all in the old dog that someone could care to share her life with me — however much of a puzzle it was.

It was the chase, however, that made this third adventure a most interesting test. There was something left of the inherent male hunter instinct in me that eventually wore down my resistance to getting close to this magical lady on whom I would set my sights.

There had been a casually polite friendship mainly of pleasantries, but conversations beyond that were haltingly brief in nature. But cautious chipping away at her carefully concealed defensive mechanism paid off. She was great at putting me through hoops and giving me just enough rope to hang on to. I could easily have construed her behaviour as bad manners but decided right from the start that I had to win.

Winning was even more intriguing when I discovered that our paths had criss-crossed miraculously in what seemed in some way that may have been willed or preordained. She appears to have been somewhere for some time like a shadow in my journeying. Many months after getting to know her, I learnt that she had been my former tax inspector at the Smart Weston Group.

Following my move into the business world, she too moved next door at Woolworth and became a regular customer. By some strange coincidence, she went into business with her late husband and, as it turned out, we both understood the pain of losing our partners at a relatively young age.

Vasantha is amusingly argumentative and a good conversationalist; she laughs heartily, in keeping with the old saying 'laughter is the medicine of life'. Oscar Wilde said 'Laughter is not at all a bad beginning for a friendship.' Vasantha's laughter certainly kindled mine and added some sparkle to my day. Before tangling into a debate with her, one had to be sure of one's facts as she will hang on to the smallest of points though they may not be substantiated. She is well-read, with an early education grounded in the rigid discipline of a Catholic institution noted for good results before going on to university where she earned a Bachelor of Science degree with a major in Zoology.

She can skate across an impressive range of subjects without deviating into the realms of small talk, which makes for a lively and interesting debate. We were agreeably, like-minded in a number of ways and everything has the strange makings of compatibility. She possesses a sharp tongue, is over protective of the one she loves, but I was soon to discover that her bark is far worse than her bite.

Pairing up was, however, not an easy decision. Several conflicts had to be resolved, the first of which was the conflict between my heart and my head, considering the failure of my second marriage. Important too, was the question of preserving my existing family relationships. My second wife had had no children and while she and my daughter by my first marriage had got on well, my son was quite a handful at the best of times and resisted the idea of anyone taking his mother's place.

A major consideration for me was whether I wanted to give up my independence again. In addition, Vasantha smoked, and smoking for me went against the grain. I could not live with someone who smoked and she understood that. So there were some pretty difficult strands of thinking to sort out, while at the same time I knew that a serious relationship outside of marriage did not fit with the kind of life I wanted to live. It was with immense delight then that I welcomed her kicking the smoking habit. It was a powerful signal that she cared and an enormous relief to me that she voluntarily removed what was for me a stumbling block.

I prayed about my other anxieties and the solution that eventually emerged was to go for an extended family out of love only, which included Vasantha's daughter Sarah who eventually became my daughter too. She was cute, mischievous and loveable all rolled into one and played a leading role in forging what was to become an all-round mutually sincere friendship. Sarah had lost her father and seemed by design to have laid claim to me as her new dad. Her coming into my life represented the fulfillment of my wish to have three children.

Her mother became my new date and accompanied me on what

was our first outing to meet with some young lawyers I was to address in Brixton. In my haste to be on time for the train, I neglected to do up the zip on my trousers. But she had noticed it as I glanced through the notes of my speech on the platform and tactfully brought this act of unbelievable carelessness to my attention. It was like a bullet to my ego. The embarrassment of it on a first date caused me to lose my cool that evening and filled me with irritation at the possible wrong message this lapse of attention might have sent to others.

It took quite some time before calm returned to my shattered pride. This incident became a light-hearted tittle-tattle she has never allowed me to forget and which, in the end, provided us many moments of hilarious laughter.

My appearance around town with a new lady on my arm at some of the many social events we attended filled the gossip columns yet again and kept folks guessing at whether I was up to no good.

As we hit the social circuit, no one enjoyed seeing the dressing up as much as Sarah did. To my amazement, she came up with a new word of her own to describe what she saw as I entered the hallway of her home to collect her mother for a ball we were to attend one evening. Vasantha was walking down the stairs in a new white designer gown specially bought for the ball. Sarah, in the meantime, had strategically positioned herself to capture my body language as I admired her mum's new outfit. Moments later, she whispered in her mother's ear that she had spotted a spink 'in my eyes'. Her powers of observation in summing up what she saw amazed me. The word 'spink' was nowhere to be found in the English dictionary. To suit her purposes, Sarah had perhaps coined a word, a cross between 'spin' and 'wink'. At age eight, she was a proper little fixer with a keen sense of interest in my reactions, which she would communicate to her mother.

She is inquisitive and hugely caring, with a deep sense of concern for the welfare of others. After watching on television the volcanic crisis in Montserrat, she took on board a fund-raising project at her school for the children of Montserrat. She baked cakes at home for sale at school and got her teachers and the whole school roped in to support the project, which raised just over £100.00.

Collecting her from school on the day of the cake sale was wonderfully touching. She could hardly lift the many heavy bags of coins which were the proceeds of the sale. She was overcome with excitement and it was our turn to reward her for a magnificent effort

159

with goodies that she enjoyed. Right from the start Sarah was to be intricately involved in our courtship and to watch her get up to her antics was truly side-spitting.

On one of our visits to the theatre I was quite late in getting away from the office and as a result we missed almost half of the show. Being late earned me a proper dressing down from Vasantha about my time-keeping. In my attempts to compensate, we dined at an exquisite French restaurant a few yards away from the theatre with a setting designed especially for lovers. Our waiter must have seen what Sarah called 'spinks' in our eyes and led us to a discreetly placed table for two. After being seated it was time to lean forward and plant a kiss on Vasantha's lips that quite took her breath away. She loved it and remarked 'I never guessed that you had it in you!' Pulling surprises out of the hat, I mused, was a natural part of this old geezer. My poking fun at myself made her laugh so much that the wine waiter was forced to back away from our table till there was calm. We fittingly celebrated with a bottle of Chardonnay.

The drama of that night out was yet to come as my silver Jag slid into Vasantha's driveway. We said our goodnights as she collected her keys from her bag and attempted to open her front door but the lock seemed to have jammed. We rang the bell but Elsie, Sarah's sitter, could not be roused. It was now 2:00 a.m.

There was only one solution. Vasantha would have to sleep at my house that night. She had the choice of sharing my bed for the first time; I could have the bed while she had the couch; or vice versa, she could have the bed and I the couch; or she could hit the floor. The last two afforded little by way of comfort especially since it was an appallingly cold night. Sorry! No prizes for guessing which option she took.

At daybreak, I drove her to the house to uncover the mystery of the locked door. The door still would not budge, so we rang the bell and Elsie came to the rescue only to find that Sarah had bolted the door after she had locked it. Turning to Sarah, her mother enquired 'why did you bolt the door?' After some hesitation, she answered, 'Well, I wanted you and uncle Tony to fall in love so I bolted the door so that you would have to sleep at his house.' How is that for a set-up by an 8 year-old?

My courting days were wonderful moments to glean and fill in blanks about the woman who was to become my wife. Under her smooth, velvety olive skin were an abundance of grace, charm and

160

loveliness that make her always fun to be with except when we go dancing. She loves dancing, especially ballroom dancing and I have to disclose, to my great shame, that she was forced to give up trying to teach me the steps. There is no question about counting my blessings at having been partnered by lovingly generous and affectionate ladies. Hopefully they too have found a few good things to say of me.

I discovered over the months of our courtship that our love for each other was not mere lust or flights of fancy, but had depth to it. Sharing and caring led to a relationship that was capable of enduring.

I was convinced that she possessed all the qualities to promote a great companionship with someone on whom I could depend. So innovative and highly gifted is she as an interior designer that, coupled with her landscaping abilities, she makes our home a place for tranquil relaxation.

I knew she had been the missing dimension in my life. Our courting days kept her in 'suspended happiness'. I discovered from early that, like most women, she loved jewelry and wanted to add a piece from me to her collection.

The time had come to invite her out shopping and to that end I gave her a budget to spend as she wished. Sure enough she headed directly for the diamond counter in her favourite store. She kept the salesgirls busy for hours. Spoiled for choice, she tried on some fifty designs humming excitedly like a kid in a toy shop. 'Do you like this one? or this one? The exercise went on and on.

By this time I wished that I could escape. She saw my fidgeting, guessed at my impatience over her indecision and soon settled on a glittering diamond she had passed over several times before. I knew she did not like my imposition of a budget, but on this occasion it was definitely my head rather than my heart that was in control. I have always held that patience is a virtue and that love has to be both patient and kind.

One week later, with Sarah in tow, she flew off to Jamaica to spend time with her good friend Norma Spence who, like herself, was a keen gardener. One morning during a gardening session, Norma spotted the sparkle of the diamond on her friend's finger and wanted to know why she had not told her of her engagement? 'It's a friendship ring', Vasantha declared. 'You could have fooled me', Norma retorted and left it at that.

When I arrived at the airport to collect them, I checked to see that the diamond was still intact on her ring finger—and it was. 'Great', I said—to see that you are still wearing it for me'. My enquiry confirmed Norma's suspicion that it was an engagement ring. The delayed announcement was made later at a private weekend party in Brighton with friends. What a celebration! We were literally washed all over with 'Bucks Fizz' well into the wee hours.

Soon after Brighton, the time had come for us to take steps to confirm our professed declarations of love. On September 3, 1992 I gallantly proposed after service on a Sunday morning and I am happy to say, was accepted without the slightest reservation on her part. Three days later we were married. The event was a closely kept secret revealed only to my secretary who would break the news to the rest of my staff after the nuptials were completed.

Keeping it simple without too much fuss was our mutually agreed way. Accordingly, a civic wedding at Enfield Town Hall on September 4 was followed by a reception for our relatives and close friends to witness the final sealing of our love for each other. The next day we flew out to a honeymoon at my private villa in Montserrat.

The new Mrs Wade disapproved of the décor and set about putting her stamp on the place. I must confess that her ideas made a difference and by then it was time to fly back home to the daily grind of steering my company.

On our return she quickly found herself alongside me driving the company, after I bought the business back from Soft Sheen. She soon became my eyes and ears, doing her bit to make things happen in the restructuring process of the new Dyke & Dryden. To her credit, it was just the kind of support that was needed to keep things on track. She became the shoulder to lean on and the ear to confide in.

Five years after we were married a trip to South East Asia was long overdue and December 1997 saw the start of an outward journey that took in Malaysia, where my wife was born, and from there on to Australia and via Singapore on the way back to London. The jaunt lasted six glorious weeks.

Our travel agents, Austratravel, had packaged every detail of our journey with the kind of preciseness that left nothing to chance. On arrival at Kuala Lumpur airport, our pickup car was waiting to whiz us off to the Federal Palace hotel and a red carpet reception, courtesy of my father-in-law, S.M. Warriar, who during his working years had earned preferential treatment from the establishment, a treatment now accorded to his daughter.

Kuala Lumpur is a world-class city with a towering skyline that speaks to its prominence as a place to do business in Southeast Asia. Seven days in the country was just enough time to whet my appetite for things to see and do.

Settling into the Federal Palace, Vasantha was visibly restless and invited me to accompany her to a nearby market. She walked briskly and as we neared a stall, she exhaled a deep sigh of relief and surged forward with urgent steps and an even louder sigh. Her 'aah' turned all heads in her direction. Her search was over. She had spotted a durian, the object of the race to the market.

It was a thorn-covered fruit, with a thick, rich off-white pulp on which she had feasted as a child and longed for. Now the feasting could begin again and she started to make a pig of herself which, in the circumstances, I understood. As one uninitiated to that fruit, I found the smell pungent and gave it a wide berth.

With her immediate longing satisfied, she purchased one more fruit and, concealing it in several layers of wrapping paper, placed it in a plastic bag and headed back to the hotel only to find that there was a ban on Durian in the hotel.

Her addiction was such that she took a chance and proceeded to the lift with the banned fruit but a porter entered the lift with us the smell gave the game away. She was advised to get rid of the fruit before the ventilating fans spread the fetid smell throughout the hotel. Trying to restrain my laughter, I was quietly relieved to be rid of the smell myself!

My wife, despite the little upset over her precious fruit, was still in sufficiently fine spirits to show me around the city. The starting point for tourists was strategically positioned adjacent to well-stocked shops of locally-made craft items whose prices, quality and presentation made shopping irresistible. All tour buses were obliged to park in the shopping precinct – a concept other countries might do well to copy.

My first outing was to visit my wife's old school that had helped to mould her character. She was particularly proud of her 50-year-old prefect badge that reads 'simple in virtue and steadfast in duty'. She had left the school with eight 'O' level distinctions. Alas, the school with its most interesting name, Convent of the Holy Infant Jesus, was nowhere to be found. A new petrol station occupied the site on which it had once stood.

Revisiting her childhood home and her father's Research Station at Seremmban was, however, still very much intact and compensated in part for the missing school. On our arrival at the compound, the name S.M.Warriar had only to be mentioned to have senior management coming forward to offer a most gracious welcome. A tour of the facility was organized, followed by what was tantamount to a banquet in our honour–a testimony to the great esteem in which Vasantha's father is held.

This leg of the journey was very rewarding–the friendliness of all the people we met warmed the heart. The butterfly, gold fish and orchid farms were wonders to behold. Here was one of the 'tiger economies' that the whole world was talking about, something of which every Malaysian must be justly proud.

Our journey continued on to Brisbane, the Sunshine Coast, and home to the Great Barrier Reef, one of the great wonders of the world that we were eventually to explore. But first things first.

Touching down at Brisbane Airport was like walking into a kind of 'space world'. Recently renovated, it was a modern showpiece of art and high tech trappings about which everyone was talking.

Members of Vasantha's family whom I had not set eyes on before were on hand to receive us. Giri Cuttle, Vasantha's sister and her husband Terry gave us a terrific welcome. Their children, young adults, Leila and Andrew were fun to talk to. They mimicked my English accent and joked about if it was it imported.

It was a great opportunity to spend quality time with my father-in-law S.M. Warriar, the distinguished agronomist who had left his mark on the Malaysian landscape. Our visits to the Federal Palace hotel and his old research establishment at Seremban spoke for him. His life stories are full of inspiration and anecdotes that keep one wanting to hear more.

His account of being captured by the Japanese and becoming a war prisoner on the same day his first daughter (now my wife) was born, is a harrowing story to say the least. His wife had no knowledge of his whereabouts for a year. Despite all this, his benevolence stands out in his forgiveness to his captors. Tending to his orchids in retirement fills him with immeasurable pleasure.

'Down under', the land of kangaroos and koala bears, is a place of immense interest. Terry Cuttle, a man of the great outdoors, had very kindly set aside part of his holidays to show us around some of the many places of interest in this vast tropical state.

The Great Barrier Reef, a heritage site was among the places underlined on our to-see list. Our visit to Lady Musgrave island was especially eventful. We chanced the crossing to the reef on a windy day and had to brave the rolling, tossing and pitching of the cruise vessel. The rough crossing was too much for Vasantha and she became terribly sick. The vessel's nurse, her sister and I did our level best to remain cool, but it was not long before we too succumbed to the turbulence of the mighty sea.

Compensating for being off colour for a while afforded the rare chance to explore and feast one's senses on the breathtaking colours between us and the glass-bottom boat in which we came face to face with a natural wonder which remains a treasured memory.

The diversity of the flora and fauna of the places we visited was breathtaking as we toured the beauty spots too numerous to mention. Crossing the enormous land mass, one could not help but notice the low price of land in the hinterland compared to that along the Brisbane River.

The Brisbane social scene was quite revealing. If you closed your eyes and listened to the music you would be forgiven for guessing that you were in Jamaica, Trinidad or Montserrat. 'Hot-hot' sung by Arrow, 'One Love' by Bob Marley, and calypsos by the Mighty Sparrow had the movers swaying and jamming.

All in all, the centrepiece of our holiday was the remarkable hospitality dished out to us by the entire Cuttle family over our four weeks in Australia. We will forever remain indebted to them.

Singapore, here we come. Well pleased with the ground we had covered thus far, what more could we expect on this final leg of a journey that had been so exciting and full of fun?

On hitting the ground, my first observation was the politeness of the customs officials and the courtesy shown by our taxi driver. He welcomed us warmly to his country and promptly announced his credentials of both driver and tourist guide. He went on to fill us in on the dos and donts and places to visit and advised that chewing gum in the country was against the law. We thanked him for his courtesy and his gummy advice.

Our arrival coincided with the Chinese New Year's Day in time to capture part of the celebrations that were taking place. The Dance of the Dragon was delightful to watch as the procession wound its way along brightly decorated streets. The dancers seemed as if they were acting out the music in what appeared to be a story of some kind. The crowds loved it and responded by clapping to the different coordinated movements the dancers made.

The emergence of Singapore as Southeast Asian 'tiger' is intriguing as is her history. Her importance as a trading post had long been recognized by Sir Stafford Raffles as agent of the East India company who later became the founder of the island state. It has been said that because of the island's strategic importance as a gateway to the Far East, it was labeled the 'Gibraltar of the East'.

Its bustling capital owes its wealth creation prowess to her fine financial institutions and the sound business acumen of her trading organizations. Her trans-shipment operations, makes her one of the world's busiest ports. As a freeport, she sees merchandise from many countries shipped to and from her shores so that loading and unloading becomes a round-the-clock activity. It is reported that in excess of 40,000 ships enter and leave her ports each year.

Singapore city boasts some most elegant structures and bears a marked resemblance to America's Manhattan. The city's jewellery stores leave the shopper in a state of confusion with the sheer variety of what is on offer. If you are a softy at heart, before going to these stores you might want to leave behind your credit card at home, or perhaps your wife!

There was a lot to learn during our short stay in this 'enterprising tiger land'. Two things never to miss—the Botanical Gardens and the food in Chinatown—the latter truly a gourmet's delight. In summary, this was a wonderful and glorious respite to which I hope to return one day.

A proud moment with Naomi.

New River Health Authority

I joined the board of the Health Authority during a period when strategic changes were taking place in the way the National Health Service was managed. The invitation to become involved in carrying out this change came as a pleasant surprise. The government of the day had taken the view that a broad-based businesslike managerial style was the one best suited to improving the productivity of the service.

This change was influenced to some degree by the success of the Training and Enterprise Councils and the way they were managed. The new organisational structure was to be in many ways similarly re-organized to model that of the TECs, with regional boards appointed to take the plans forward by calling on the proven skills of people who had worked in a similar environment. It was hoped that this move would infuse a spirit of change within the Health Service as the TECs had done for industry.

The recruitment task force for the Health Authority Board in the boroughs of Enfield and Haringey, well aware of my public involvement, short-listed me as one of the board's representatives. The matter of short-listing, on the one hand raised questions about what I could bring to an organisation dealing with matters relating to health of which I knew little or nothing; on the other hand, it also offered the possibility of overloading myself with responsibility.

At the interview, I duly raised my fears about my unsuitability in matters dealing with health. I was quickly reminded that my inclusion was intended to allow me to bring my local knowledge and management experience to bear on improving the working arrangements in a businesslike manner. With that said, the interview proceeded and my name was subsequently submitted to regional head office. Later, a letter arrived confirming my appointment as a director of the New River health authority, including my time requirement and a salary package.

Shortly after, a mass of paper work arrived containing the agenda for the first board meeting together with a glossary of acronyms that were in part the language of the health authority. The ordeal of committing these to memory was somewhat frightening, but fortunately over time they fell in place without too much bother.

My induction and welcome on the board was full of warmth, thus putting to rest my own misgivings about the new assignment. It was cushioned by the fact that some of the faces were familiar, including its chairman, who had been my old boss at the Training and Enterprise Council and knew of my commitment to giving my best shot at anything undertaken.

The key positions on the board were appropriately filled by health professionals whose responsibility it was to feed into the new management regime information on the competing health needs. It turned out that budgetary control was to be central to the management of scarce resources across the authority's many spending agencies. Efficiency savings were part of the grand new design and business leaders were to be instrumental in bringing about this change.

Primary and secondary care, together with preventative medicine and the citizen's charter were items at the core of driving this change. The jury will in all fairness be out for at least two or three decades on a decision on how measurement of performance will demonstrate whether gains made have compensated for the effort and time spent in driving changes forward.

I had a choice of the areas in which I might work and settled for a spell in public health, under the guidance of the authority's director of environmental health.

My first assignment was a look at the persistence of low morale among staff members at all levels of the organisation. After a discussion with the director of personnel, I was given the go-ahead to speak with staff members and was soon to discover that discontent was mainly due to a failure to communicate the rapid rate of change taking place within the organisation. My recommendation to the personnel director was that staff be removed over a number of weekends and a facilitator hired to update everyone on what was happening and, more importantly, why. She agreed, but then the problem was raised of how the authority was to meet the fees for a consultant in the absence of such funds. Putting on another of my public hats, I suggested that she leave the matter to me a little longer while I sought a source of funding.

Wearing my training and enterprise hat, I brought the difficulty to TEC board's attention and succeeded in getting agreement for the funding. My recommendation to remove the staff was off to a flying start.

The programme proceeded over several weekends away as was suggested. At a subsequent authority board meeting the personnel director reported on the results of the change. To the delight of the whole board, my suggestion had worked and the staff was adopting a happier frame of mind. This met with a round of applause from members.

Tony Felix, the chairman, known for not losing momentum, at once turned to me and enquired what was next. The next steps I responded without hesitation, was that we should become an investors-in-people organisation. In the same breath, I turned to Jeff, our chief executive, and asked whether we had his commitment. His reply was a quick and confident 'yes'. That meeting represented a turning point in the authority's staff relations.

Experience gained in this field was invaluable in giving me a better understanding of how our health service really worked and of the sacrifices that being made by an army of dedicated health professionals and supporting staff in keeping the service functioning. Visiting wards and making assessments of service levels, listening to complaints at health council meetings, attending youth health education seminars, keeping a watching brief at mental health clinics, or simply trying to understand the difficulty in reducing patients' waiting lists at board meetings, or pronouncing on grievance interviews, were only some of the many assignments that had claim on my time.

It was for me a most satisfying chapter in my journey and a truly wonderful experience to have served the health service in this way. It was interesting to find that at the end of my three-year contract, the region wanted me to carry on. I was unable to meet this request as a new and significantly larger assignment awaited me, to take forward namely the redevelopment of Stonebridge Estate in the Borough of Brent. The following is an acknowledgement of my services to the authority.

The Management Team

Antthony Wade
Chairman

Sorrel Brookes, Chief Executive

Nick Coates
Director of Finance and Administration

Christine Morris
Director of Development

John Brewster
Director of Housing Management

Michael Pierce
Director of Employment and
Social Regeneration

My management team that changed the
face of Stonebridge

171

The Re-development of Stonebridge

July 30, 1993 marked the beginning of yet another challenging assignment. A letter arrived that day from the department of the environment which read, 'I am writing to confirm my secretary's call to you about your meeting with officials to talk about the Shadow Chair appointment for the proposed Brent HAT (Housing Action Trust).' That meeting took place on August 9, at 2 p.m. at the department's offices.

A further letter dated August 24 slated a meeting for September 15 with Sir George Young, the housing minister, to discuss my appointment to the post. The meeting went well, for his officials had already done the groundwork and my interview with Sir George was merely for his political endorsement and for him to personally put across to me some of the things that he wished to see taken care of.

He wanted, for example, to be sure that the appointment of senior managers of the Trust reflected the racial mix on the estate and that women had equal access to management positions. I assured him he could count on me on those two views that we mutually understood. A starting date for the post was subsequently confirmed for November 10 that year.

I had met Sir George Young socially before and had formed an opinion of him as a genuinely nice person and a good party man whose politics I guessed was in tune with the one-nation philosophy. I was delighted to discover that this was indeed so.

The importance of the appointment was not lost on me, for it was the first such senior appointment of a black person to the chair of a non-departmental public body. It was certainly a massive challenge in terms of scale, for inner-city deprivation and the many social problems attached to the area were massive.

Clause 60(5) of the Housing Bill which specified the role of

HATs read: '...to carry out a major programme of renovation, in consultation with the residents; bring empty council properties back into use; improve the way estates are looked after; and generally help to improve the economic, environmental and social condition of the area.'

My initial response after the confirmation of my appointment was to visit Stonebridge, speak to residents and try to get in tune with the tempo of the place. The estate lies in the heart of the Borough of Brent, just minutes from Wembley Stadium and the Park Royal business park. It covers an area of 77 acres, with a population of 5,000 in 1,750 homes built in the postwar years of the early sixties and seventies which reflected the cumulative problems arising from the prevailing poor construction processes of the time.

The homes were mainly high-rise, panel-built blocks dotted across the estate and had really had their day. Evidence of despair and neglect was everywhere and a negative perception hung like a cloud over the place. On my first visit I used a black taxi-cab to take me to the estate. To my utter amazement, the cabbie dropped me off outside the estate adjacent to the blocks, swearing that he never ventured into the grounds. Had he had a bad experience with the place, I asked. His reply was no, nor was he about to have one. He wished me good luck and hurried off. This then was the public perception of the Stonebridge estate.

In the meantime, my first priority was to put together a shadow board and a team of professional advisers in preparation to kick-start the project. Richard Compton, the official at the Department of Environment (DOE) was my sounding board and was always on hand to point me in the right direction.

Lucy Robinson, a senior civil servant, was seconded to be my shadow chief executive/chief accounting officer. Lucy and I made a great team and had many things in common. She was a skilled negotiator with a persuasive charm that worked wonders getting results in many a sticky situation. Her grasp of what needed to be done, her team spirit and commitment quickly bolstered my confidence in her judgement. Quite clearly we were often of like mind and her uncanny ability to read my thoughts amazed me.

Richard Compton had provided us with a list of possible candidates from the private sector that I might interview to fill the key professional board positions. Having perused the lists, we made arrangements to interview those we considered suitable candidates. In so doing we were mindful that our own success in meeting our remit would depend to a very large extent on the people with whom we surrounded ourselves. We were therefore as thorough as we could be. After our interviews the selected candidates were run past Richard Compton who agreed with our choices. This signalled for us a good start.

Our next step was a major test in getting the project off the ground with the residents of Stonebridge. A meeting had to be scheduled to advise them of what government had to offer and the partnership role that the estate was expected to play in the proposed HAT project. We were advised that there were a number of residents hostile to previous approaches made to bring about change on the estate and that this might prove a difficulty.

Indeed, political suspicion was rife. Residents, despite their poor housing conditions, were avowedly pro-Labour and wanted nothing to do with a Conservative government whom they believed would deprive them of the security of tenure so far enjoyed. At the same time, an extreme left-wing element wanted nothing to do with change, as their trade of evil flourished in the environment that prevailed.

A date and time were arranged to meet with the members of the Stonebridge Tenants' Advancement Committee (STAC) to get to know each other as a start to our discussions. Whether by design or because of a failure to observe punctuality, the Chair of STAC was quite late in arriving. He finally turned up, carrying a large collection of books under his arm as if summoned to court. There was no greeting and he appeared somewhat irritated as he spotted another resident in attendance at the meeting. 'What is that fellow doing here?' he demanded. 'Is he not a resident?' I enquired of the committee. They all replied that he was. 'That being the case, he has every right to be present,' I responded.

The Chairman, Mr Clement Beadeau, collected his thoughts and invited his committee to leave the meeting with him. Lucy turned on her charm and somehow between us we succeeded in convincing them that it was in their best interests to stay and hear what was on offer. They stayed, and that night represented the beginning of a dialogue that set wheels in motion for the HAT.

Thus the preparatory work in moving matters forward from our end was off to a fine start. The shadow board was in place, minus the resident board members who were to be elected after the ballot if a 'yes' vote was achieved. We were now in a position to ask STAC to arrange for an estate-wide meeting at which to present the board and its brief on the proposed redevelopment of Stonebridge.

A good representative number of residents turned up for the meeting, and most of them welcomed what we had to say and were delighted by the presentations, especially those given by the two members of Brent council whom they trusted. Represented at the meeting also was DOE that held the purse strings and had oversight for the project.

As might be expected, the meeting generated many questions, chief among them being: Will this really happen? My short answer was yes, provided there was a 'yes' vote. I then went on to explain that because of the guarantees given in the Housing Act of 1988 which covered the areas of security of tenure, right to buy would be the same as it would if the council were to develop the estate; that housing benefits would continue to be available and that all secure tenants could vote in a ballot, with the HAT consulting tenants after it had set up its proposals.

Additionally, I continued, there are assurances given by government ministers which can be relied upon, such as: rents would be frozen until works on homes was completed; money would be provided for redevelopment or refurbishment and three members on the HAT board would chosen by residents. These were but a few of the issues to be expected which had been carried out by other HATs before us and would be circulated on 'fact sheets' to every resident of the estate.

The existing sensitivity and mistrust called for extreme care about being impartial, providing only facts and leaving residents to make up their own minds.

The work was exhausting, but at the same time exhilarating, with each new chapter as interesting as the one before. In an effort to accommodate residents' working hours, our meetings were always held in the evenings and sometimes lasted long into the night.

As Chairman, and in a bid to build confidence, I had let it be known that my Chief Executive or myself was always available to answer any questions on which residents were not clear. This worked well for the genuine callers, but became a nightmare for others who would always awkwardly choose the most inconvenient times to call. It was, however, the nature of the job and, once committed, there was no turning back.

Our many meetings and discussions had by then taken us to the point of organising the ballot that was to decide the future of the estate. A secret ballot was organised to take place from March 14 to 27, and was to be carried out by the Electoral Reform (Ballot Services) Ltd.

Nothing was to be left to chance and a strong campaign got underway for the minds and hearts of the residents. CHAT, our in-house magazine the voice of the proposed Housing Action Trust, swung into action. Below is the text of my message to the residents:

> 'I want to take this final opportunity before the ballot begins to give you some very personal views and promises.

> As Chair of the North London Business Development Agency, an organisation I helped to set up using public money provided by the government, I have helped more than 1,300 new businesses get started in North London. So I am no stranger to making government funds work for communities.

> When I speak to people living outside of Stonebridge about Stonebridge, I hear about a place where nobody would want to live — a place that they think is so bad that it becomes difficult to understand how anyone survives there!

> But Stonebridge is not like that. Stonebridge has been put down for far too long. I want to help to show that Stonebridge is a strong community ready to take its future into its own hands. With up to £100 million in public money, Stonebridge can become a community where you, its people, really enjoy living, and to which those on the outside will look jealously.

> But there are some people on Stonebridge who remain suspicious and others who say they can't be bothered. To those people I would like to make some

personal promises. I promise that if the HAT is voted for, it will involve Stonebridge residents in all major decisions, and will consult extensively on all changes to the estate.

Knowing only too well how important employment is to the regeneration of Stonebridge, I promise that the HAT will make employment creation a top priority; will result in more jobs for Stonebridge people; and will ensure that the right training is available to give residents the skills needed by employers in the area.

Homes are at the centre of the HATs' remit. I promise that everyone entitled to vote in the ballot will get a new or improved home and that when the work is complete, rents will be pegged to those for similar council properties in Brent.

Finally, some people have said that the HAT is a private landlord. This is not so. It is funded by public money — a one-off opportunity to change your lives with no risk; no loss of benefits; no change to your security of tenure; and with a legal right to return to the council. This is really your opportunity, to shape your future.'

The outcome of the ballot was a pleasing success for those of us who worked hard to make it happen, despite a very strident anti-HAT competition throughout the ballot. The size of the 'yes' vote made it particularly gratifying, a whopping 68 per cent was by any standards a major achievement. Here I pay tribute to everyone and especially to Lucy Robinson, my secondment from the Department of the Environment and my Deputy Chairman Clive Lloyd, CBE, our famous captain of the West Indies cricket team. They together with Lucy's staff were the backbone of our campaign. Clive's celebrity status was a winning ticket with residents.

With the ballot now behind us, we moved from our shadow status to full designation as Parliament passed the 'Designation Order' clearing the way for the HAT to make good its promises to residents during the ballot. In the meantime, recruitment for a chief executive and supporting staff to implement the project was underway.

Sorrel Brookes, a no-nonsense person, beat the field as the successful candidate for the posts of Chief Executive and Accounting Officer, assumed office in December 1994. She brought to the table a wealth of experience from her previous twelve years in senior management positions at Manchester's council housing department. The ball was now in her court to select a staff that would become the core management team to pull things together. The team was made up of a director of finance and administration, a director of development, a director of employment and social regeneration and a director of housing management.

Selecting the master planners was our next formidable task – one that would test the credibility of the HAT to its fullest. Uppermost in my mind all the time was the fact I knew that the greatest care had to be taken to ensure that we appointed the best people we could possibly lay our hands on.

Choosing a master planner is a tough job. In the first place, the job had to be advertised throughout the European Common Market. Our advertisements attracted some 102 expressions of interest. Merely sorting and responding to these presented a major task. In the end, five teams were shortlisted after eleven months of intense consultation. The teams selected were then put through the rigours of individually providing: an exhibition of their proposal and a presentation to residents. They were subjected to a long and detailed interview by a representative panel at which they were asked to provide written proposals and a costing price for the job. It was only after meeting those exacting requirements that the final selection was made by the board.

But this final selection was not without its problems. On October 19, an estate-wide meeting to present the team chosen was hijacked by a disgruntled group of residents including a resident board member who felt that a black firm should have been engaged for the job. The carefully planned meeting was thus turned into a circus of confusion.

The uproar left me no option but to adjourn. After consulting with the board, a new date of October 23 at 8 a.m. was agreed to resume where we left off. Members all arrived at the appointed time only to find on arrival that the locks were all super glued and the building surrounded by the same group that had caused the disruption of the night before.

We kept our cool and were not to be deflected from our hard-won democratic responsibility to the majority of the residents of Stonebridge. Steps were taken to remove the encumbrances as, with some difficulty, we pressed on with the job at hand of agreeing the selection of the master planners. This action sent a clear message to the fringe group of activists that their disruptive antics were not going to be tolerated.

The culprit who caused this bother was a resident board member. He was a man prone to complicate the simplest of issues merely for the hell of it. He would challenge where there was nothing to challenge. It was part of the make up of the man. In an effort to tame him and to demonstrate the transparency of our actions, I invited him to be part of the development committee responsible for selecting the master planners. He was party to the selection of the team that was eventually agreed yet when I came to signing off on the agreement, he sought to undermine it. It took the constancy of Job to deal with him. Steps to reduce the possible damage his actions might create were immediate and the following letter was despatched and circulated to all residents across the estate:

Dear Residents,

I am very pleased that the Board has decided who should plan the new Stonebridge. It's taken a long time and a lot of hard work to reach this decision, and it's been a difficult choice to make.

I know that some of you have concerns about the HAT's selection process. I also know that there has been some misinformation and confusion about what the master planners will be doing. I hope the information you get in this issue of CHAT will clear these problems up.

I am confident that we have made the right choice. Some people have asked me why the HAT has not appointed a black-led team. The answer is that we have appointed the best team for the job. Stonebridge is a multi-racial community and we have chosen a multi-racial team with both black and white staff.

This doesn't mean that the HAT isn't taking notice of residents' concerns about appointing black professionals to work on Stonebridge. The HAT is working hard to find ways of getting black professionals to tender for work, so they may be role models for all our people, black and white.

I am sorry that a minority of people have disrupted the selection process. I know that most of us are keen to get things moving on the estate. I hope that now we have a clear decision, residents will work closely with the master planning team to design the new Stonebridge.

Sgd. Tony Wade, Chair.

Fearful that despondency could easily set in as a result of the long wait between drawing up the plans and getting work in progress, an initial community needs assessment survey was carried out as a first step toward moving to alleviate some of the estate's most acute problems.

In the interim, the poor state of many homes on the estate required urgent remedial work and a 'catch-up' programme was commissioned to spend £1.3 million on repairs and the monitoring systems, making a noticeable difference to the place. It was but a small beginning of things to come.

There was also visible change too in attitudes, and how best to harness this occupied my thoughts for some time until one day the penny dropped. A sublime message might well be one of the answers I thought, and so it was. During an estate-wide meeting I invited suggestions for a slogan (with no names added) by which to live and work.

The meeting turned out to be most receptive to the idea and, that evening, everyone was invited to put suggestions in a box. Out of the audience came a question directed to me — 'What about your suggestion?' I was moved by the question for although I did want them to own the slogan, I could certainly not hesitate to be part of Stonebridge, which indeed I was.

Subsequently, a committee was put together to pick what they considered to be the most appropriate slogan and, as it happened, mine was the one that was picked: WORKING TOGETHER FOR A BETTER STONEBRIDGE. This slogan became part of our corporate identity and was used in our letterhead and on all the HAT's promotional material, including the banners placed in the main community meeting rooms as a silent reminder of our message and mission. All the evidence has suggested that it made a difference.

Stonebridge was never going to be an easy assignment, that it would be a challenge was putting it gently. However, despite the problems, we remained steadfastly focussed on our goals and objectives and by the year 1996/97, my last in office, I was able to summarise our achievements with some satisfaction. The following is a summary of my report:

> 'It is with great pleasure that I introduce the Stonebridge Housing Action Trust's (HAT) latest annual report. I believe most residents would agree that last year saw us translating our watch-word "working together for a better Stonebridge" into fact. We worked closely with residents and other partners to start bringing about lasting change in Stonebridge and have achieved many of the year's targets ahead of schedule.
>
> We laid the foundations for the redevelopment programme by agreeing with residents on a master plan and appointing architects to design the first 700 homes, which will help to remove the obstacles which prevent Stonebridge people getting and keeping jobs.
>
> We continued building positive relationships with employers, and supported residents through further

education and training, employment guidance and better childcare provision.

To achieve our aim of providing high quality housing management, we took over direct control of the service from Brent Council and worked with residents on ways of improving it. We hope this will create a more positive feeling on the estate and enhance our credibility.

Last year, we also continued our work with residents, community organisations and local agencies to improve community, youth and leisure facilities in Stonebridge, and tackle some of the causes of social and economic deprivation. We awarded 35 grants to organisations ranging from a lunch club for elderly people to a drug-education project.

We also continued to build partnerships with agencies that are already, or are willing to become, stakeholders in the Stonebridge future. This will help ensure that our achievements are sustainable and that we develop appropriate succession strategies. Our partners so far include local businesses, shopkeepers, the local authority, the Tec, local nurseries, Parkside Health Authority, Harlesden City Challenge and Park Royal Partnership.

HATs provide a unique opportunity to regenerate an area to a high enough standard and across the necessary range of activities affecting quality of life, to result in sustainable outcomes. In Stonebridge, we are tackling one of the UK's most difficult areas, where the problems residents have are complex. There is no quick fix; achieving real solutions takes time, energy, commitment and cooperation from residents and partner agencies, as well as significant investment.

We are still a long way from completing our work in Stonebridge. However, we have already achieved some notable successes and started building effective working relationships with residents, their representatives and our partners.

Our success so far is due in part to hard work, commitment and the support of many people, and I would particularly like to thank the HAT staff team, the HAT board, the residents of Stonebridge, the department of the environment and the government office for London. Stonebridge HAT made good progress in 1996/97 and I look forward to building on this in the years to come.'

This chapter of my journey has been exceedingly rewarding in the knowledge that under my leadership, and with the support of many stakeholders, the project has made and will continue to make a difference to the quality of life of thousands of its residents. It is also gratifying that I was able to deliver on the solemn promises made and remain thankful for the trust the people of Stonebridge have placed in me.

During the consultations, I recall being questioned by a small group of residents about the validity of my promises. I referred them to their 'RED' document (residents' expectation document) and to their 'independent tenants' friend'. Yes, they said, but at the end of the day if things go wrong, it is you that we shall hold responsible. It is heartening that things did not go wrong for those who had placed their faith in me.

On the wall of my office at home, a collage presented to me on leaving occupies pride of place. On the front is a collection of the many phases of the development depicting a hive of activity in which I was involved with residents. On the back of that elegant and expressive work of art, the picture is decorated with symbols of heartfelt good wishes and gratitude. This for me remains a most exquisite and touching gesture from the Stonebridge people who I know asked for nothing more than equality of opportunity and a chance to be seen as people playing their part in helping to build a better society.

Angela Eagle, Under-secretary of State for the department of the environment summarised how I had fared at Stonebridge. The following is an extract from her letter:

> 'I would like to take this opportunity of thanking you very much for your invaluable contribution to the Stonebridge Housing Action Trust during your time both as Chairman of the shadow board and of the full board following designation.
>
> You accepted the challenge of leading the shadow board at a difficult time in the history of Stonebridge when the residents, having seen the quality of life within their community deteriorate, were very sceptical of any new proposals to regenerate the estate. Your determination to gain their confidence and to explain clearly and concisely what the option of a HAT would mean for them, was instrumental in achieving a clear "yes" vote in the subsequent ballot which led to the creation of the HAT.
>
> During the first three years of the HAT, you have successfully taken over the total management of the estate and introduced programmes of repair and maintenance that have made an immediate impact on the quality of life on the estate. An imaginative programme of community projects has been introduced and residents now have direct access to education, training and job-seeking so important in establishing a self-reliant community. But most important of all, you have led the residents through the long and difficult stages of creating a master-plan for the redevelopment of the area which we are all about to see turned into reality with the beginning of the first stage of building.
>
> You must feel justly proud of the progress you achieved during your period as Chairman and I know that I speak on behalf of not only the board of the Trust and the senior management of the HAT, but

especially for the residents of Stonebridge who have much to thank you for.'

I welcomed the minister's factual statement, but it would be remiss of me not to say that I had a fundamental disagreement on a matter of principle with the Minister at the end of my contract. The outgoing Conservative government, after a thorough investigation, accepted the board's recommendation that the troublemaker should be relieved of his position.

With the intervention of 1997 general election that decision had to be postponed until the election was over. In the interim, the board member who had caused no end of problems resigned. The Conservatives lost the election and the new Labour minister, on visiting the estate, sought my views regarding him. I told her that I stood by the recommendation the board had made.

Angela Eagle in whose gift it was to appoint or dismiss a board member refused to act on the board's recommendation and this created an impasse during which three board members handed me their resignations rather than carry on working with a bully she was aware of my intention to resign and carried out what I might call 'a political ambush' by advising me that she had decided not to reappoint me before I was able to hand her my own resignation.

Events that followed proved that we were right to have had the guts to act on what we knew to be the correct course of action and not to drag our feet. It was this approach that made things happen for Stonebridge! The Minister, on the other hand, with no understanding of the situation on the ground, sacrificed principle for some unexplained political expediency and reappointed the bully – an approach, in my view, that was bad for democracy and evidence of a most disgraceful behaviour on the part of the Minister.

That said, what worked for me was the trust and confidence that the people of Stonebridge had placed in me. I was able to empathise with them and felt deeply about being part of the changes that were taking place.

At the invitation of Ian McDermott, Chief Executive, I visited the New Stonebridge in August 2004 to see at first hand the progress that had taken place since I left. It allowed many residents the opportunity to share their sense of pride in what had been achieved.

As I was shown around the completed stages and saw the smiles on the faces of all I met, I heard repeated the same story of their deep satisfaction at the outcome — new, comfortable, well-designed homes with beautiful gardens were everywhere to be seen. Mick McDonald who in the early days had challenged my promises showered me with praises. It was a moment of great joy for me to see the expectations of the people of Stonebridge fulfilled.

On July 26 2007, I was grateful to have been invited to share in the HAT exit celebration party for a project that is regarded ' as one of the leading regeneration success stories in the whole country'. This has been for me, a truly fulfilling spell of service to the Stonebridge community.

I am grateful to have been part of that change.

The Montserrat Volcano Trust Fund

Moving from one project's hot seat to yet another has not been uncommon in my journeying. Vacating the chair of the challenge of Stonebridge for that of the chair of pulling together support for a volcano-devastated Montserrat was nothing new.

What was different was the catastrophic nature of that destruction. The scale of relief required called for massive aid from governments in concert with world organisations. The agreed brief by the West Indian Standing Conference was to do anything possible that would help to bridge the gap in the suffering that had visited the island.

Support by family members and friends was miniscule considering the magnitude of the disaster, but it was the kindred spirit that stirred Montserratians in Britain and their friends to band together to do their level best to support our brothers and sisters back home, that made the hot seat bearable.

The conference had devoted one of its monthly meetings to drumming up nationwide support for tackling the crisis. It was at this meeting that I was invited to become the chair for the Montserrat Volcano Trust Fund.

The media duly gave widespread cover to the emergency, but many of us felt that the debate was not taking place where it should be — on the floor of the House of Commons. This discussion was in our opinion a top priority. The way of fast tracking the subject was, in my view, to raise a question in the House at 'question time'.

Contact with known members of the House who could raise the question was of paramount importance. In a conversation with Janice Panton, Chair of Mac 89, it transpired that Dr Ronnie Cooper, one of the first persons to be caught in the blanket of fog and with first hand experience of what had happened, had made it to London and related his epic story to Mac 89.

There were a number of parliamentarians personally known to

me and I suggested to Janice that I was minded to first approach Dianne Abbott, the Member for the London Borough of Hackney and see whether she would be willing to raise the matter on the floor of the House.

I subsequently telephoned Dianne and asked if she would be willing to see us for a first hand account of what had happened from Dr Cooper. She was most receptive and agreed to see us immediately. We met her at her home one Sunday evening and on the following Monday afternoon, Montserrat was on the floor of the House.

It was the first shot in what was to become an ongoing debate that speeded up action on the island. Our lobbying had worked and full credit marks went to Miss Abbott. She subsequently followed up and was a strong supporter in applying pressure on the Foreign and Commonwealth Office to get things done.

We were now on course for getting our message across in the places that mattered. Fellow Montserratians and their many friends around the globe were linked in spirit by the destruction and especially those who had visited our once safe and peaceful sanctuary.

Montserrat Overseas Progressive Alliance (MOPA) and Mac 89 based in London with other groups in Birmingham, Slough, Leicester and other parts of the country all rallied to give their support to the national efforts in their respective ways in combating the crisis.

Independent of the British Government's schemes for the island, the Montserrat community groups in the UK had moved to found the Montserrat Volcano (UK) Trust Fund on October 27, 1997 in the House of Commons to coordinate a programme of assistance for the people of the island.

As Chairman of the Trust I recall my opening remarks that evening: '*it was for us all a defining moment in time, which brings out the best in each of us; it acknowledged our common interdependence on each other; it represents the brotherhood of man in action as we go about giving hope to our brothers and sisters on our volcano-troubled island.*

Our aim was to do our best to convert tragedy into hope for the future, and to demonstrate to ourselves as well as to the world that it is possible to transcend appalling circumstances and constructively rebuild our lives and what is left of our island into a new invigorated and resourceful Montserrat.'

The theme of my speech reflected the views of everyone present.

We knew that it was of the greatest importance that we keep alive an awareness of the scale of the catastrophe, and the Trust throughout 1998 succeeded to a large degree in maintaining public awareness of the continuing problems on the island.

In December of that year, an account was opened at the Bank of Montserrat in the name of the Montserrat (UK) Volcano Fund and a local committee was formed to distribute the sums of money that became available. Eleven families were among the first to benefit from the Trust's efforts.

Rudi Page of Statecraft Consulting and I held the view that it might be possible to mobilize support from Southern Ireland (the Emerald Isle) because of the special relationship with Montserrat. With this in mind, and at our own expense, we made our way to Ireland to explore how we might best take this idea forward.

After watching the film, 'The Other Emerald Isle' by which Montserrat is known, it occurred to us that hooking up with Michael D. Higgins, the Irish sociologist who had made the film could be a powerful ally in helping us to fulfil our objective.

On the first day at the hotel at which we stayed, Rudi Page picked up a magazine lying on the coffee table in the room and opened it at random. He gasped loudly. To his utter amazement, on that random page was the picture of Michael D. Higgins the eminent sociologist as large as life in a feature commending his contribution as the government minister concerned with Irish artistic development. It was quite miraculous, and we could not help but conclude that this had to be divine intervention!

Our findings were quite exiting. On our return, we reported to the management committee the outcome of our trip and recommended that our visit had made it clear to us the correctness of pursuing the strategy we had undertaken. The committee sanctioned our recommendation and started to mobilize support through our awareness strategy for our group to spearhead a visit aimed at re-establishing our links with Ireland.

Next steps were to advise the government and people of Monserrat of our intensions and to that end we visited the island to explain our plans as to how we proposed to proceed. Governor Abbott, Chief Minister Brandt and his administration welcomed our visit, wished us well and gave our plans their blessings.

At a reception hosted by Governor Abbott for Rudi Page and

myself in thanking him for his hospitality, I joked that there was no need to apply the Lord Tebit 'loyalty test' to him on which side he was batting for, as we knew by his Herculean resilience in the face of the crisis, that he was batting for the people of Montserrat. (The loyalty cricketing test is determined by which side you clap for when England is playing the West Indies in England.)

On our return to the UK, reconnecting the two Emerald Isles was now firmly on our agenda. A date for the visit was agreed for August 5, 1999. It turned out to be a history-making journey for 32 Montserratians led by myself touched down in Dublin where we were received by our tour guide. We checked in at the Green Isle Hotel just outside the city centre. The trip was full of interest, fun-packed with plenty of excitement as we journeyed to Galway, Limerick and Cork. Included in the group were Chief Minister Brandt, members of his administration, the Montserrat Credit Union, the Montserrat Chamber of Commerce and the Tourist Board.

The visit turned out to be a great success in meeting our initial objective of opening up a new dialogue, to pursue issues which, if managed well, we hope will continuously provide mutual benefits for both countries.

There is a strong sense on the part of the Irish that they should explore the section of their history and they were very receptive to rebuild on the ground-work carried out by the Trust. This opening represented a tourism opportunity. It was a question of how the Montserrat Tourist Board would exploit it. There were also huge benefits by way of educational opportunities, skills transfer and trading links, which we hoped would flow from the Trust's efforts of reconnecting the two Emerald Isles.

Throughout our travels, we were graciously received and made headline news across the news media. A headline article in one of the popular daily papers, the 'Conncht Sentinel', read: 'The Other Emerald Isle pays Galway a visit'. The subheading of a full page covering our mutual history, spoke of the lost Galway Tribes' links to an island in the Caribbean!

These statements by the press in my view represented an invitation to the Irish community at large to explore the roots they had put down in the Other Emerald Isle.

The Montserrat Oriel String Band was part of our visiting group and shared in the annual International Feakle Festival. The Oriel band set the festival alight as they pitched in with authentic Irish music to the delight of the crowd. Most of us came feeling that the event invoked a strong sense of belonging. A clear basis for reconciling the past exists and the event demonstrated to us without a doubt that the special bond is real enough!

Michael D. Higgins, T.D., the distinguished Irish sociologist, in his documentary on Montserrat, showed due regard for the sufferings of Montserratian slaves. During his visit to the Plymouth cemetery, he declared: 'The graves in this cemetery carry names like Riley, Ryan, and Sweeney, names as Irish as the Shamrock and therein lie the bones of slaves who toiled for Irish masters that bear testimony to a strange past, hidden or forgotten, where many were to die bearing the names of their oppressors.'

This was a statement of fact he highlighted showing his own remorse about it. On our final night, Michael D. Higgins was duly honoured by the group for his work in rekindling the spirit of friendship that exists between our two countries.

Much has transpired as a result of the Trust's initiative, and it remains to be seen how Montserrat will continue to take forward the new opportunities created and work with the Irish Republic in the years to come.

The new constitutional status of the 14 remaining overseas territories is, in my view, to be welcomed. This change calls for the creation of a representative parliamentary framework around the centre which needs to be transparent and grounded in the spirit of partnership which will enable overseas territories to engage in and contribute by open debate on issues that affect them as a group. A move in this direction will give credence to the British sense of fairness and will be an important brick in the building of a truly inclusive society.

One good example of the need for such a body can be seen in the slow pace of handling the Montserrat volcano crisis due to lack of representation, before it was raised on the floor of the House of Commons.

The Montserrat Community Support Trust

The MSCT was yet another project linked to the volcano crisis on the island and the resettlement of some of its people in the United Kingdom.

The brief of this body which I was invited to chair differed however from others in scope. It dealt specifically with meeting the immediate resettlement needs of Montserrat evacuees unsettled by the volcano crisis. This project was supported by the Home Office Department for International Development (DFID).

The Trust's main areas of responsibility were to engage in the resettlement of evacuees with access to education, housing, DSS/welfare benefits, immigration status and social fund/grant applications. Under the dedicated leadership of Lazelle Howes, the Trust's Chief Executive, with a small committed staff and a team of volunteers, was instrumental in delivering some hard-won gains to benefit the Montserrat evacuees. This made it possible for the Trust to succeed in meeting its resettlement targets in the above areas.

The nature of the work was such that it called for long hours, well outside the norm. It was only through this type of commitment that the Trust could submit in its annual reports results that demonstrated its outstanding achievements. These included developing community networks by channelling resources to community groups and volunteer programmes; by directing and assisting people to have access to higher education and employment; by promoting and supporting sporting activities; by monitoring and promoting the health of evacuees; and by the preservation of our history and culture.

In my message in the annual report for the fiscal year ending 1999, I spoke for the board and reflected the view of all our people associated with the Trust in my statement appended below:

> 'I am delighted that I had the privilege to lead the Montserrat Community Support Trust during its first and very critical year of operations. MCST has been at the centre of the process of adjustment for Montserratian evacuees now consolidating their resettlement into the UK society.

As we reflect on the experiences of our people over the last five years, it is clear that the challenges facing a displaced community such as ours demand that we empower ourselves to cope with an increasingly dynamic situation.

The challenges we face force us to focus on whatever the obstacle, be it immigration, education or any of the other diverse issues facing evacuees in Britain.

We are a people proven to be generally up to the challenge of turning around circumstances stacked against us, and capable of fashioning our own programme for development and success, by designing and promoting opportunities for the exposition of our creative abilities.

Montserratians in the United Kingdom are, I believe, unified in purpose and fortified with hope. It is with a sense of great pride that we reflect on the past, with confidence in the potential within our community to face the future. In conclusion, to serve my island in this role has been for me a great privilege.'

Change in Ethnic Advancement

It is my considered opinion that no other community has blended so well into the multicultural landscape of Britain as have settlers from the Caribbean. We are often described as a likeable, cheerful, friendly and hardworking people who share a common language and, to some extent, a similar cultural background with white Britons. This is the inevitable result of a history which, though often turbulent and conflict-ridden, has nevertheless produced a rare and rich cultural synthesis of African and British values.

Nowhere is this cultural unity better reflected than in the marvellously fertile field of literature dominated by such highly accomplished writers as Walcott, Selvon, Lamming, Salkey, Naipaul, Matura and scores of others. Indeed, in qualitative, stylistic and technical terms, many writers from the Caribbean have not only greatly enriched English literature, but have also changed its hitherto Eurocentric face. English literature is no longer the preserve of the indigenous English.

Almost the same humanising, progressive process has revolutionised British art, aesthetics, music, song and dance. The people from the Caribbean brought with them a music that has helped create most of the ingenious innovations by which recent generations of youth who infused a more universal dimension. Popular dances, too, have captivated the nation, uniting black and white.

The greatest single contribution of the settlers was the gift of Carnival which, in the face of many difficulties, still endures. It is now a loved and indispensable cultural institution. Nor has black influence been lost on what became the swinging sixties, the decade that ushered a new sparkle into the British psyche.

Most of the older generation, men and women, were cricket mad. Many of the survivors of that age still are. The younger generation is less passionate about cricket, yet it is generally expected that young

British sportsmen of Caribbean origin will shine with the same lustre on British cricket fields as some of our illustrious predecessors, led by the legendary Sir Learie Constantine, intellectual and diplomat.

While some young British-born cricketers made their mark in county and national cricket, many have consciously turned their backs on cricket to embrace football. It was the right decision, indeed a commercially and socially shrewd one. Cricket may be the game of the establishment, especially of the public schools and the remnants of the landed aristocracy, but its financial rewards are relatively small.

The big money is in football and some of the highest earners in the game – people whose incomes are sizeably more than that of many in the city, in business and industry – are young West Indians and Africans. They have read, and continue to read, the situation with the astuteness of mature business people judging by the burgeoning number of very able footballers in Britain today.

Strangely, when people talk about Afro-Caribbean business, they seem to forget that professional black footballers, athletes and sporting people in general are also business people. Indeed, if one were to produce an Afro Caribbean rich list, one would be pleasantly surprised by the impressive number of soccer millionaires in a game not noted for the articulacy of its players.

Black football commentators and analysts are much in demand by the media. One of the much-loved stars, the witty, effervescent and knowledgeable Ian Wright, hosts a talk show of his own. Garth Crooks, the very respected BBC sports commentator has also served football in many outstanding areas.

Most of the earliest settlers, people from rural agricultural backgrounds, regarded commerce as a risky proposition. Others from Christian backgrounds viewed usury and sharp business practice with distaste. Content with their reasonably well-paid jobs and trouble-free lifestyles, they were the backbone of the emerging black middle class in Britain, in terms of standard of living, especially car and home ownership, consumption, entertainment and savings. We are, comparatively speaking, as good as all the other emigrant communities of about the same period.

That is not to say that the small-business sector totally lacked participation. Some dynamic Caribbean women struck the first blows. They quickly saw an opening in black hairdressing salons and stepped in with courage, skill and vision. Black hairdressing and the black cosmetics industry remain among the most important sectors in Britain in which the community has a stake.

An interesting feature in the forging of this development was the consciousness of the hairdressers. Without degrees in business administration, they operated by instinct and were intelligently media-wise. They spent a fair amount of their income advertising in black newspapers, especially the *West Indian World* whose finances were shaky because of lack of advertising support from corporate Britain. Sadly the paper folded, but its legacy was formidable.

Out of its ashes was born a new generation of newspapers, especially the bold campaigning *Caribbean Times*, edited by Arif Ali. Aubrey Baines who founded *West Indian World* had lit the torch and a visionary Arif Ali nurtured the sacred flame for well over a memorable decade and a half championing black causes.

The *Caribbean Times* was in many respects credited with setting the black political agenda and succeeded in doing so because of its editorial integrity, its unique analytical style and its unquestioned status as the political voice of the black community. On the burning issues of the day, it was compulsory reading for progressive British politicians.

One example that stands out is the labelling of the ANC as a 'terrorist' organisation by some right wing papers, offering support for the odious apartheid regime. The *Caribbean Times* was the only British newspaper to expose the horrors of apartheid and to campaign unequivocally for isolation of the Pretoria regime.

Events since stand in judgement of the correctness of the paper's steadfastness in its campaigning policy. The moral strength of a community exercised through its newspaper must never be lost on the generation to follow. The paper's influence on change was enormous. Black small businesses benefited from the paper's generous credit-tolerance and sympathetic discounts, thus encouraging entrepreneurship and playing a significant role in the pursuit of wealth creation in the community.

Wealth creation by black business people is now an indisputable fact, and I quote from the recent 2004 ground-breaking research carried out by Eric Osei, Senior Business Development Manager of the London Development Agency, supported by a Barclays Bank report that reveals that the majority of new business start-ups are by people from ethnic minority backgrounds – a large proportion of whom are black.

'Black-owned businesses now generate a combined annual sales of £10 billion and employ 100,000 people. Coupled with the £4.5 billion spending power of London's black community, African and Caribbean people are wielding increasing economic power.'

Nowhere, however, is black advancement more pronounced than in the professions, coming as it does from the second generation of highly educated individuals that now stretches across almost every discipline, in medicine, accountancy, law, the arts, music, the social services, education and others with a fair progressive movement into the civil service.

This integrated movement into the mainstream has taken time and is most certainly a great credit to those families who have pushed and steered their offspring into becoming achievers. Clearly, the groundwork is steadily being laid for assuming and sharing in the processes of nation building for tomorrow.

A pertinent observation that characterised black advancement in Britain was that black people had the vote and the right to exercise it. There were, and still are, attempts by some extreme right wing elements to disturb and stir up trouble in what today remains one of the most tolerant nations of the world.

One is mindful that the temptation to stir up trouble came also from an attempt in the 1960s, by the Black Power Movement in America to export their philosophy into the UK. The British black settler is essentially conservative and rejects extremist movements. There was no place for a Black Power Movement in Britain and its less than a hundred vague and confused followers soon dissolved into nothingness. Constitutional political debate and a resounding declaration of support for the ballot box followed.

This eventually produced a number of councillors. One of the first to influence political change was Basil Lewis, OBE, who became the first conservative councillor in Hornsey, a true blue constituency. Basil's win made a statement that represented the political aspirations of the community.

He represented the constituency for 16 years until he retired. During that time he fostered the community's awareness of its political strength. From this pivotal position he was instrumental in the founding of the Anglo-West Indian Conservative Society and became a successful lobbying force. Among that society's many successes was its campaign for the removal of the 'Sus' laws, which affected the black community indiscriminately. Introduced by Home Secretary Willy Whitelaw, they gave the police authority to carry out random search of anyone suspected of crime.

Several parliamentarians were to follow. One of the pioneers was the late Bernie Grant, a highly successful and powerful orator and an uncompromising opponent of unfairness. Bernie refused to be shackled and stood his ground to the last. His death at the height of his political prowess was an irreparable blow to progressive British political change.

With more and more well-educated, committed and dynamic young people coming through with their eyes on a political career and driven with a passion for service, we may well see some interesting developments in coming decades. Borrowing the late Prime Minister McMillan's famous phrase, the wind of change is all around us and in some small way it has been wonderful for me to be a part of it.

Winding Down

Interestingly, several companies in my industry had designs on the Dyke & Dryden brand. It meant, therefore, that making my exit from an activity in which I had been engaged for over three decades was not too difficult to deal with in terms of converting my assets to cash.

However, tearing myself away from what had become part of my life for all these years called for a tough mental resolve. A deal was done with a South African group of companies in January 1998. The new owners softened the pain of my exit by offering a retention contract and an ambassadorial role that served the interests of both parties.

In much the same way as with the sale to Soft Sheen in 1987, questions kept cropping up as to why I had not sold the company locally. Sure enough, I can empathise with people who felt that way, for it was the way that I had felt to begin with, but clearly, with my previous experience now behind me, it had to be simply a question of 'seekers and finders' and 'let market forces prevail'.

Experience tells me that you do business with your head and never your heart for chances are, by doing business with your heart, you could so easily find yourself ending up with heart failure.

Capitalism, I strongly believe, is the greatest of all economic systems; trying to buck the system serves no useful purpose and only leads one up a blind alley. My own attempt in following a course contrary to the views I have just expressed was for me a particularly high price to pay. Money knows no colour and business should always be done according to the rules of the market.

In giving up employment, I must confess that there was some anxiety as I contemplated my next step in filling what I thought would be long hours of boredom. I was soon, however, to find out how wrong I was in entertaining that thought even for a moment. To my utter disbelief there was equally as much call on my time as when

I was fully employed. The big difference was being able to work at a more leisurely pace and at times of my choosing.

The year 2000 saw me settling into a new routine with some speaking engagements and the writing of my first book, *How They Made A Million—the Dyke & Dryden Story* published in 2001. Jotting down my business experiences of all those years was, in a way, living it all over again. It was a pleasant, fulfilling and effortless piece of work and full of enjoyment, made more so by receiving positive comments from readers from a wide cross section of society.

Among the many acknowledgements and speaking engagements to come my way, one in particular filled to a large extent my hopes and wishes for the black community's ability to build on its strengths. It was the invitation to use my book in the Business Workshop presentation as part of the inspirational session for the Black Heritage Conference on October 23, 2002 organised by the Mayor of London at Congress House, Great Russell Street, London WC1.

The conference theme – 'Living Histories: Marking the Past, Building the Future' was positive and unmistakeably clear about the messages it was transmitting to the huge invited audience. The messengers were the offspring of legendary heroes who had fought for justice, for fairness and respect.

They were Mr Tusher Ghandi, great grandson of Mahatna Ghandi; Ms Zindi Mandela, daughter of Dr Nelson Mandela; Ms Yolanda King, daughter of the late Martin Luther King Jr – all touch bearers, who amplified the moving spirit of the conference with their presentations on how they were building upon the work of their forebears. That I was invited to lead the business seminar in this line up was an indescribable privilege.

My second book, *Black Enterprise in Britain* has come on stream on a subject which, hopefully, will find a place in many homes, schools, and libraries. This work seeks to enlarge people's understanding of black people's contribution across the society at large in which we live and work.

My journeys across West and East Africa have been a notable experience in discovering and coming face to face with my heritage and the opportunity of being schooled in the richness of black culture. This discovery is one which I hope more people from across the diaspora will have an opportunity to explore and share.

The feeling of being spiritually at home wherever I went on the great continent of my ancestors, was as it were akin to a mystical baptism. It was a necessary homecoming event that led me to kiss the ground in celebration when I first touched down at Murtala Mohamed international airport in Nigeria in 1982.

Since that time I have made several visits and made many good friends in what is now for me another home where there is always a warm welcome. As if to confirm that seal of belonging, in March 2003, I had the signal honour of being made a Fellow of the Elegant Twins School of Cosmetology in Nigeria at a double celebration, her golden jubilee—in marriage—and in business. (1953-2003). What a track record for Elizabeth Osinsanya! What an institution and a fortress in her profession! I salute her and was overjoyed to be present at the ceremonies.

While I have been graciously received in all my travels across Africa, Ghana has left its mark on me by the warmth and homeliness with which I was showered. The cultural courtesies and kindness with which visitors are received is something I shall always remember.

Ghana's history means much to me, especially since it is said to be the land of my 'roots', although I have so far been unable to discover exactly from where my ancestors hailed. One thing is certain, I instantly connected and felt very much at peace there.

The stories of the 'drum roll', the call of the Ashanti Kingdom, are fascinating, as are also the stories about the 'Golden Stool', said to be the symbol of power of the Ashanti. Legend has it that around 300 years ago one of their wisest and greatest priests called together the Ashanti in an effort to unite the nation. He commanded from the sky a symbol that would get them together. Amid thunder and darkness there descended a golden stool to land on the lap of the priest.

I must admit that I find the story full of mystery and will one day I hope learn more about this revered object. I must disclose herein, that I am the proud owner of a gift from a dear friend of a replica of the stool that is now among my trophies.

I want to acknowledge on this page that it is the strength of these many friendships that I have made both in my personal and in my business life, and community involvement, that has been the bedrock of support that has seen me through the ups and downs in my journey. Neither time nor space will permit me to mention the many kindnesses I have received along the way for which I am eternally grateful. But a few that have been really enabling in my journey will perhaps suffice.

The Most Excellent Order of the British Empire (MBE) awarded for my contribution to employment by Her Majesty the Queen in 1987 remains a proud moment in my journey. Of equal importance too, and with a deep sense of humility, was 'An Evening in tribute' on June 30, 2000, organised by members of the black community to celebrate how they felt about the company's efforts in the struggle for economic liberation. I quote below extracts from their letter of June 5 in which they wrote:

> 'The background to the event to which you are invited is that we feel that our community should have the opportunity to honour our pioneers, personalities and activists during their lifetime and to provide inspiration for other generations.
>
> The evening will focus on the contributions made by the company and its directors both in spearheading a successful business venture during harsh times and against the tide, and in nurturing other businesses and cultural activities. We anticipate an evening of celebration which will be both nostalgic and inspiring to present to up and coming black business persons and other members of the community.'

Another event of equal importance to which I was invited was the UK Trade & Investment Black Enterprise Awards 2005, at which my company was nominated for an award. The presenter, Maggie Semple, expressed her thoughts thus about the ceremony:

'Ladies and Gentlemen,' she declared, 'this evening has made me very humble. To have an idea and turn it into a business is a major achievement, but to grow a business into a sustainable company is an even greater achievement. We all know the challenges of starting up a new business and all of tonight's nominees have demonstrated that they have done so successfully.'

The Lifetime Achievement in Business Award goes to an entrepreneur or group who, in the opinion of the judges, is a pioneer, a person who has paved the way for many and who has been in business for at least 10 years.

The nominees she named were: Chinwe Studios, Dyke & Dryden and McDonald's Restaurant.

Each of us nominees, I knew, was gripped by the same nervous tension as the audience hushed in anticipation as Maggie opened the envelope. 'It gives me great pleasure to announce that the winner of the Lifetime Achievement in Business Award 2005 goes to Mr Tony Wade of Dyke & Dryden.'

The room erupted with applause as I joined Maggie on the platform. In true Oscar style, cameras flashed as Maggie handed the award to me. It was a truly humbling moment.

Among my other awards are: the Caribbean Times Award 1984, ZiZ Promotions Award, 1985-86, the Caribbean Afro Society of Hairdressers Award, the Business Federation Enterprise Achievement Award 1990 and 1999, the Gleaner 150 Years Special Merit Award for Business, the Voice Citation 1992, the Sunrise Golden Award and a Proclamation issued by Atlanta City Council for establishing business relationships between businesses in England and Atlanta. These honours have all been received with a deep sense of humility and appreciation.

Industry Appreciation

Acknowledgement of the company's pioneering role in ethnic business development continues to be recognised. In 2007, Salon Strategy, the professional body representing the hair and beauty industry at its annual conference generously extended an invitation to me (all expenses paid) to be their special guest of honour on Friday

January 19, to celebrate the pioneers of the industry. This was yet another humbling experience in my journey.

To be invited to an event at City Hall, the seat of London government, was by itself a signal honour and so too were the arrangements for an evening that could not be faulted. I was completely bowled over to find that the front covers of two books by pioneers on both sides of the Atlantic were skilfully contrived to carry the programme for the evening's event. The two titles were that of beauty products pioneer, Madam C.J. Walker and the Dyke & Dryden story.

On Her Own Ground by A'Lelia Bundles tells the story of her great-great grandmother. The late Madam C.J. Walker, entrepreneur and philanthropist, who pioneered the world-famous Walker cosmetics company in the US in the nineteenth century, is pictured above at the wheel of one of her vintage cars. Below, my late business partners Len Dyke and Dudley Dryden stand with me as pioneers in the industry in Britain during the twentieth century.

A unique feature of the reception was the showing of a short pre-recorded film of interviews by a number of the guests who were known to me or had worked with me over the years. Their comments were particularly revealing of the high esteem in which my colleagues and I were held.

Event organiser Anne Long–Murray, CEO of Salon Strategies, echoed the feelings of many present: 'I'm glad we decided to honour these heroes, to highlight the incredible contribution they have made to entrepreneurship in the black community and the legacy they have built for thousands of people now employed in this industry. The racism they faced is almost unbelievable, compared to the issues black businesses face today. It's still not easy, but we are so much further ahead now because of their sacrifices.'

Although I knew the company had touched the lives of many

people over the years in so many different ways, the full impact of what we had done only consciously registered and sank in that evening.

The many tributes make it difficult to distinguish between them, but one in particular stood out and meant a lot to me. Gary Gardener was the former President of Soft Sheen Inc, and now President of Namast'e Laboratories. His vision for our work together had an unfathomable depth as no one knows that better than I do.

> The following is an extract from what he had to say. 'I am so proud to be able to join you in honouring the life's work of Mr Len Dyke and Mr Dudley Dryden--God rest their Souls—and of my good friend Tony Wade. These gentlemen have taught me so much. First and foremost, they have taught me character and integrity. They were giants, not only in this industry, but in their communities on both sides of the Atlantic, and Tony Wade's vision and tenacity has yet to be surpassed.'

It was also wonderfully gratifying to meet with A'Lelia Bundles, author and journalist who presented me with a copy of her critically acclaimed best-selling biography *On Her Own Ground*, the life and times of her great-great grandmother who built a beauty empire, amassed unprecedented wealth and devoted her life to social activism.

That the charming and talented Miss Bundles should come to London to be the keynote speaker for an event in my honour, is a distinction for which I am eternally thankful.

Other notable guests that crossed the Atlantic for the occasion were Mr Larry Mallory, Vice President of International Sales & Marketing, of Pro-line Corporation, Mr Ned Washington Jr., Director of Sales at Avlon Industries Inc., Mr Fred Luster, founder of Luster's Products, a formidable American product manufacturer and his dear wife Precious Luster, Director of Logistics at the company as well as Mr Reginald Maynor, their International Director of Sales & Marketing.

It was especially heart-warming to hear from young business executives, Kikora Mocka-Celestine, now International Marketing Manger at Proline Corporation, who cornered me and thanked me for gaining her entry into the industry to work first as a model, and from Derrick Williams, owner of the famous 'Trend Exclusive' of Stoke Newington, London. The latter greeted me with penetrating warmth. 'Your company,' he said, 'was like a stone which when dropped in a pond of water sent up ripples everywhere.' Thanks and blessings to them all.

I have, throughout my entire business life, always contended that the success of my partners and myself in business had much to do with the partnerships we built with our community, one which our community aspirations and dreams were much the same – a means of working to release ourselves from economic domination and of trying to achieve economic liberation. And, while we are not quite there yet, one thing has happened for sure. The company has pointed the way ahead. Thankfully, our efforts in serving the community and our country have made a difference.

It is difficult to include the many friends and well-wishers who have supported me personally in ways too numerous to mention. A few selected letters from a cross-section of society will, I hope, illustrate my working relationships and are attached on the following pages.

Finally, I acknowledge my many blessings, give God thanks for his goodness and great mercy, and pray for his continued blessings and divine guidance in all that I have done and am yet to do.

Appendix 1
Selection of Congratulations

MOPPA
(U.K.)

Montserrat Overseas Peoples' Progressive Alliance

46a Lydford Road, London, W9 3LX   Tel.: 01-969 9707

General Secretary: Jane O. Furlonge, 11 Kingsdown House Amhurst, Road, E8   Tel.: 01-254 5707

Please quote this reference
on all correspondence

22 June 1987

Mr A E S Wade
44 Queen Elisabeth Drive
Southgate
London N14

Dear Mr Wade

I am deeply pleased to be afforded the opportunity to extend on the behalf of the Executive and members of the Montserrat Overseas People's Progressive Alliance, our congratulations to you on your being awarded the MBE in the recent Queen's Honours, in recognition of your services although to the business community in the main, but more importantly, in our estimation, to the black business sector.

We feel confident that you will continue in your usual unselfish way to expound the many attributes of our people in this society.

Our best wishes to you and your family in all your endeavours.

Yours sincerely

W I Trant
DIRECTOR.

jvp/II/32

Minister of State

Department of Employment

Caxton House Tothill Street London SW1H 9NF

Telephone Direct Line 01-213 ....5949.......

Switchboard 01-213 3000

Anthony E S Wade Esq MBE
44 Queen Elizabeth Drive
Southgate
LONDON
N14 6RD

24 June 1987

Dear Mr Wade

I was pleased to see your name included in the recent Birthday Honours List and am writing to offer my warm congratulations.

Although I have only recently taken up responsibility for Small Firms issues, I heartily endorse this award. Small firms play a key role in the continuing growth and success of the nation's economy and I am pleased to see entrepreneurial success recognised in this way. I find it particularly commendable that although fully occupied with the expansion of your own firm into the export market, you have contributed generously of your own time and energy to help set others' feet on the business ladder.

I whole-heartedly applaud this award and understand that it was fully endorsed by both the Home Office and the Department of Trade and Industry. I would like to wish you every success for the future and trust you will enjoy your forthcoming investiture.

Yours sincerely

JOHN COPE

From the Director General

RECEIVED - 1 JUL 1987

30 June 1987

RECEIVED - 1 JUL 1987

A E S Wade Esq MBE
Dyke & Dryden Ltd
19 Bernard Road
Tottenham
London
N15 4NE

Dear Mr Wade

I was very pleased to read of the great honour that the
Queen has bestowed on you and I send you the warmest
congratulations of all of us here at the Institute of
Directors.

Yours sincerely

SIR JOHN HOSKYNS

RECEIVED - 2 JUL 1987

Business in the Community

227A City Road
London EC1V 1LX
Telephone: 01-253 3716
Facsimile: 01-253 2309

President: HRH The Prince of Wales

Mr. Tony Wade MBE,
Managing Director,
Dyke & Dryden,
18 Bernard Road,
London,
N15 4NE.

Our Ref: RSOB/pd
29 June 1987

Dear Tony,

I wanted to add my own note to the large number of congratulations you will have been receiving over the past few days. I was absolutely delighted to see that you had been honoured. Your contribution, both through your own business and through the Enterprise Agency movement has been really important and I am so glad that it has been recognised.

Please accept the warmest congratulations from all of us at Business in the Community.

Yours ever

STEPHEN O'BRIEN

Appendix 1

Shell U.K. Limited

Shell-Mex House Strand London WC2R 0DX

A.E.S. Wade Esq., M.B.E.,
Chairman,
Dyke & Dryden Ltd.,
19, Bernard Road,
Tottenham,
LONDON,
N15 4NG.

Telephone 01-257 3571 direct line
or 01-257 3000   switchboard
Telex 22585 Shell G
Fax group II/III 01-257 3920
Telecom Gold 81:SUK 001
our ref   UKPA/21
your ref
date   16th June, 1987

Dear Tony.

    I am happy to join the avalanche of congratulations which are daily arriving in the post for the civil honours that you have received in recognition of the work that you have done in the area of creating worthwhile opportunities and rewarding work for a great deal of people over the last few years. I am delighted for you - the honour is well merited.

Yours

Telephone
01-499 8600
Cables
JAMHICOM, LONDON, S W 1

JAMAICAN HIGH COMMISSION,
50, ST. JAMES'S STREET,
LONDON, SWIA IJS.

26th June, 1987

Dear *Mr Wade*,

It gives me great pleasure to extend sincere congratulations to you on behalf of myself and members of staff of the Jamaican High Commission on the award of the M.B.E. for outstanding achievements in the Business sector.

Your dedicated services to the business community as a whole, your personal contribution to the firm of Dyke & Dryden Limited, and your work with the Black Business Organisation in particular, have been acclaimed and the honour is richly deserved.

I am certain that you will continue to be a source of inspiration to the community in the years ahead.

Again, sincere congratulations and best wishes.

Yours sincerely,

H. S. Walker
High Commissioner

Mr. Tony Wade, M.B.E.,
c/o Dyke & Dryden Ltd.,
19, Bernard Road,
London N15 4NE.

Appendix 2
Music Sheets and Treasured Moments

Everything

Tony Wade

Say That Again

Tony Wade

2. Love is a song two hearts must sing
   Love is the world's most wonderful thing
   Even in the night all the world seems bright
   From the moment you whispered "I love you".

3. All of my life was lonesome and blue
   Hoping and praying my dream would come true
   You called my name and my heart burst into flame
   The moment you whispered "I love you".

Honey Bee

Tony Wade

2. I love you so much, don't know why
   Don't think of leaving, you'd make me cry
   Take my heart, take the key
   Oh oh oh you honey bee.

3. Oh oh oh you honey bee
   Just what happens when you kiss me
   You thrill me so much in all you do
   All my lovin is just for you.